The Sacred Diary
of
Adrian Plass (aged 37¾)

The Sacred Diary
of
Adrian Plass (aged 37¾)

Adrian Plass

Marshall Pickering

Marshall Pickering
34-42 Cleveland Street, London, W1P 5FB

Copyright © 1987 by Adrian Plass
First published in 1987 by
Marshall Morgan & Scott Publications Ltd

Reprinted: 90, 91, 92:
Impression number 15 14

British Library CIP Data

Plass, Adrian
  Sacred diary of Adrian Plass
  1. Youth — Religious Life
  I. Title
  248.8'3'0924 BV 4850

  ISBN 0-551-01418-0

Text set in Baskerville by Brian Robinson, Buckingham
Printed and bound in Great Britain by
Courier International Ltd, Tiptree, Essex

Diary—A. Plass

Saturday December 14th

Feel led to keep a diary. A sort of spiritual log for the benefit of others in the future. Each new divine insight and experience will shine like a beacon in the darkness!

Can't think of anything to put in today.

Still, tomorrow's Sunday. Must be something on a *Sunday*, surely?

Sunday December 15th

Another commercial Christmas! I shall send only ten cards this year. What is Christmas about, after all?

Our church is getting like an auction room. One blink and you get ministered to. Sit still and keep your eyes shining—that's my motto. This morning was Edwin Burlesford's fault. Forty-five minutes on 'sin'! A record nine-fruit-gum talk. Halfway through, I was checking supplies when Edwin suddenly shouted 'LUST!', and made me drop the packet under my chair. Put my head down between my knees to locate it, then couldn't get up because Doreen Cook pressed her hands down on the back of my head. She prayed that 'our despairing brother would move from darkness to light'. I was all for that—I couldn't see a thing. When she let me get up she had one of those roguish Christian smiles on her face. Came very close to really giving her something to forgive me for. Everyone thinks I've got a big lust problem now. At coffee time they all smiled reassuringly at me. Leonard Thynn hugged me. I signed Edwin's carol-singing list for next Saturday to show that I'm not all bad. Gerald's coming too.

Monday December 16th

My son Gerald says James Bond is on next Saturday evening. Pity it clashes. Still, carol-singing is the Lord's work.

Absent-mindedly bought a box of 50 Christmas cards. Never mind—that's enough for five years.

Tuesday December 17th

Dreamt last night that I *was* James Bond.

Wednesday December 18th

Is carol-singing scriptural? Rang Doreen Cook's husband, Richard, who thinks Christmas trees are wrong. No luck—apparently it's okay.

Bought another 50 cards.

Thursday December 19th

Could it be that God's trying to say I *should* watch James Bond? Opened my Bible at random and put my finger on the page. It said,

'The dogs licked up the blood'.

Went to bed. I don't understand God sometimes. . . .

6

Friday December 20th

Laid a 'fleece'. If a midget in a Japanese admiral's uniform came to the door at 9.04 precisely, I would know that God wanted me to sing carols.

9.05: A miracle! No-one came. That's that then. Leonard Thynn came at 10.30 selling charity cards. Bought 50.

Saturday December 21st

What an evening!

7.30: Film started. Surprised to find Gerald settling down to watch. 'What about carol-singing?' I said. 'Oh, no', he replied, 'I rang old Edwin on Monday and told him there was a good film on, so I wouldn't be going'.

Why don't I do things like that?

8.45: Edwin at the door, concerned as I hadn't gone carol-singing. Lost my nerve and told him I was still fretting over my lust problem.

11.00: Edwin left after counselling me for 2¼ hours. Missed the end of the film. As he left, Edwin said, 'I'm off home to watch that Bond film. The wife's videoed it'.

Gerald said it was the best ending to a film he'd ever seen. He grinned in a rather unchristian manner when he said this. He's a good lad though. Patted my head and said he thought God liked me despite everything.

Next year I am not sending *any* Christmas cards.

. . . Despite what???

Sunday December 22nd

Guest speaker at church today, dressed in a monk's

habit. He said that God is nice and he likes us. Everyone looked at Edwin to see if we agreed. Difficult to tell as he was grinning like a happy little boy. Speaker kept quoting Mother Teresa of Calcutta, who is, of course, a *Roman Catholic!!*

Afterwards, Richard Cook whispered to us, 'Ah yes, but is she saved?'

Gerald whispered back, 'Ah yes, but how many filthy beggars have you washed this week, Richard?'

Anne said she thought the monk was wonderful, so he probably is.

Had some news today that would be really depressing if we weren't Christians. Anne's Uncle Ralph, who is the most vulgar man I have ever met, will have to spend Christmas with us. Wouldn't be so bad, only we've already got my Great Aunt Marjorie staying from tomorrow. *She* condemns wine-gums for their 'intoxicant potential'! Gerald rubbed his hands when he heard the news.

Oh, dear. . . .

Lay awake for a while thinking about what the monk said. 'God is nice and he likes me.' Felt oddly peaceful.

Monday December 23rd

Met Gerald in the hall when I got back from work. He said, 'The Titanic has docked.'

Found Aunt Marjorie looking through the TV magazines in the sitting room. After we had exchanged the customary kiss in which not even the tiniest part of my face touches the tiniest part of hers, she said, 'I am encircling with black ink, those programmes that are unsuitable and which we shall *not* be watching during the Christmas period!'

Gerald poked his head round the door, and said, 'There's a man at the door with a deliverance ministry.'

Turned out to be the postman doing a late round. A parcel and two cards. Counted the cards we've received so far after everybody had gone to bed tonight. Not as many as last year. Naturally, I forgive all those who've forgotten us, but you'd think they could make a bit more effort. After all, that's what Christmas is all about, isn't it?

Uncle Ralph arrives tomorrow.

What on earth will Marjorie make of him?

Gerald says he makes Bernard Manning look like the Archbishop of Canterbury.

Talking of Gerald I've decided I must *do* more with him. He's asked me to go along on Friday to hear the new Christian music group that he's formed with a few friends.

They call themselves 'Bad News For The Devil.'

I *shall* go.

I like music.

Tuesday December 24th

How is it possible for someone like Anne to have an uncle like Ralph? He arrived just after lunch, a short, very fat man, on a tiny motor scooter. Life is just one big whoopee cushion to Uncle Ralph.

Disastrous first encounter with Great Aunt Marjorie. Kissed her full on the lips, and said, 'No-one told me there was going to be some spare talent on the menu this Christmas. Stick around Marjy-girl. You could be right up little Ralphy's street!'

Aunt Marjorie turned puce, and has refused to look at him, let alone talk to him all evening, even when he

9

flicked through the Radio Times and said, 'Heh! Good biz! Someone's gone through and marked off all the best progs!'

Anne and I arranged all the presents under the Christmas tree tonight. The ones from Uncle Ralph are all shaped like bottles.

Asked Anne what she thinks God loves about Uncle Ralph. She said, 'His niece.' Kissed.

Wednesday December 25th

Christmas Day!

Aunt Marjorie went off to a 'proper church' this morning.

Ralph not up by the time Gerald and Anne and I left for the Christmas service.

Enjoyed it all very much except for a point halfway through the prayer-time, when George Farmer, who was sitting behind me, stood up and began to swing his fist from side to side as he prayed fervently for good will among God's people.

Suddenly felt a heavy blow on the side of my head and slumped forward, momentarily stunned. Shook my head to clear it, and realised to my amazement that Farmer was still ranting on as if nothing had happened!

Didn't feel much good will.

I said to him afterwards, 'I forgive you for punching me in the head, George.'

He said, 'Did I really do that?'

Gerald said, 'Yes you did. It was on your twenty-fifth "just"—I was counting.'

Went home.

Spent the rest of the day rugby-tackling Uncle Ralph's jokes before they could cross the line. Became more and more difficult as he drank more and more whisky.

After tea, he went up to his room to get something 'really good' for a game he knew.

Came back with a rubber monkey attached to a long length of elastic, and told Great Aunt Marjorie she should stuff the monkey down her dress, pull it out at the bottom and pass it to him so that he could put it down his trousers, then pass it to Anne.

Thought for a moment she was going to faint.

She retired to bed early, leaving the bottle of gin that Ralph gave her this morning, unopened in the waste-paper basket near the foot of the stairs.

Gerald, who seems to have enjoyed the day enormously, asked Ralph if he knew any more 'good games'.

Ralph said the best game he knew was one where you sit in a circle and each person drinks a bottle of whisky, then one person goes out of the room, and the others have to guess who it was.

How can you run a Christian household with people like Uncle Ralph around?!

I could be a really good Christian if other people didn't mess it up all the time.

I've noticed this before.

Mentioned it to Anne in bed tonight.

She said, 'Well, I promise you, darling, that Gerald and I will try really hard not to stand in the way of your saintliness'.

Just a hint of satire there, I fancy.

Thursday December 26th

Richard Cook turned up this morning to invite us to the Fellowship New Year's Eve party.

Talked in the kitchen.

Dreaded Uncle Ralph appearing suddenly and saying something really awful.

Afraid I wasn't altogether honest.

I said 'Anne's Uncle Ralph is staying with us this Christmas, Richard. He's not a Christian, and he can be—well—let's say, difficult, but I honestly think part of our witness has to be showing a spirit of tolerance, and perhaps even giving the impression sometimes that we enjoy or laugh at things that might be—well—not quite on'.

Said this because I hadn't been able to help laughing at one or two of Ralph's dirty jokes, and knowing him he was quite likely to say to Richard, 'Here's a good one! Adrian nearly wet himself when he heard this one!'

As for witness, it never crossed my mind in connection with Uncle Ralph. Not the Christian type, I suppose.

Amazed when we took our coffee into the sitting room to find that a miracle seemed to have happened. Ralph shook hands quietly and politely with Richard, and insisted on leading him to the most comfortable chair, saying, 'It's a real pleasure to meet one of Adrian's friends. Do sit down.'

As Richard put his weight on the chair, a most awful noise came from underneath him. Shot to his feet again, and Uncle Ralph lifted up the cushion to reveal a deflated rubber bladder with the words 'A REAL BRONX CHEER' printed on the side. Ralph was in hysterics of course.

Richard, obviously taking to heart what I'd said in the kitchen, started to cackle in his high-pitched artificial sort of way, and said, 'Oh, what a good joke against me! I don't disapprove of it. Oh, no! I think it's very funny. Ha, ha!'

Very ashamed.

Rang Richard later and confessed I'd not been very truthful.

Give old Richard his due, whether it's thick skin or love I'm not sure, but he doesn't bear grudges.

Told Anne and Gerald what had happened when they came in.

Anne, who'd been out on a disapproval tour of the area with Aunt Marjorie, was rather short with me.

Gerald made me tell him what had happened three times over. Could still hear him laughing hours later when we were all in bed.

Thank goodness Marjorie and Ralph are leaving tomorrow.

We've all had enough really.

Twinge of toothache tonight. . . .

Friday December 27th

They've gone! Peace again.

Went to Unity Hall tonight to hear 'Bad News For The Devil' practising. When I got there, stood outside for a moment listening to a noise that sounded like a piano falling down a lift-shaft with someone trapped under the lid.

Turned out to be a number called 'Peace Will Come'.

Privately thought a better name for the group would be 'Rather Encouraging News For The Devil'.

Didn't say so though.

They're all very keen.

There's Gerald on the lead guitar, Vernon Rawlings on bass guitar, Elsie Burlesford on flute and

William Farmer on drums (very loud), and vocals (unintelligible).

Turns out none of them are even *remotely* interested in fame or riches, only serving God through music.

Never seen Gerald so earnest about anything.

Edwin's invited them to play at the service in three weeks 'if they're ready'.

Hmmm. . . .

Saturday December 28th

Toothache slight but persistent.
Anne mustn't know!

Sunday December 29th

Got up.
Toothache.
Went to bed.

Monday December 30th

The lights are going out all over my head!

Tuesday December 31st

Awake at 5.00 a.m. with this blasted toothache. Gloom! Prayed hard in the lavatory. Maybe it'll just go away. Getting more and more irritable. Must be careful or Anne will guess.

To the Cooks' at 9.00 p.m. for the Church's New Year's Eve party. Earlier on I had said, 'We'll take quiche, shall we?'

Anne said, 'Cake would probably be better.'

Gently reminded Anne that scripture tells us the man is the head of the woman. We took quiche.

Everyone took quiche! No sandwiches, no cake, no puddings, just acres of—quiche.

Anne said, 'What now, oh Lord and Master?'

Gerald said the Lord's Prayer should change to 'Give us this day our daily quiche, because that's all Christians ever eat.'

Richard Cook was standing nearby and overheard. He said it was mocking the Word, and did Gerald really have assurance?

Gerald foolishly replied, 'Yes, I'm with the Woolwich.'

Richard stormed off towards the raspberryade. I wish Gerald wouldn't do it.

Left after an hour or two of loud embarrassing games organised by George Farmer.

In the garden on the way out, we found Leonard Thynn having a theological debate with a large garden gnome, and drinking something from a Tizer bottle. Took him home, Gerald insisting on staying to see him in and put him to bed. Typical Gerald. Not religious, but nice.

Wednesday January 1st

1.30 a.m. Anne's gone to sleep. I can't. My jaw's on fire!

Might as well write down my two New Year resolutions:

(1) *Every* morning—take Anne a cup of tea in bed. She deserves it.
(2) *Every* morning—have quiet time after making tea. Give God more of my time. He deserves it.

10.00 a.m. (at work) Disaster! So tired after sitting up late mulling over my resolutions, I forgot to set the alarm and we all overslept. Anne was very angry with me. Gerald grinned in that maddening way he has. Late for work. No quiet time.

Toothache's awful, but I feel the Lord is saying, 'I will heal you. Don't go to the dentist.' Prayer is what's needed. (Taking pain-killers until prayer is answered.)

Thursday January 2nd

Toothache BAD!!! Wife ugly. Son ridiculous. God non-existent. Quiet time? Early tea? Huh! Why doesn't God heal my tooth if He's so wonderful? Pockets awash with empty pain-killer packets. I think Anne suspects.

Friday January 3rd

PAIN! PAIN! PAIN!

Richard round tonight, apologising to Gerald for losing his temper on Tuesday. Then Gerald apologised for making him lose his temper, then Richard apologised for not coming round sooner, then Gerald . . . etc, etc. So ridiculous! *They've* not got toothache!

Afterwards, Gerald said that an apology from Richard was like GBH from anyone else. Felt a sudden, excruciating twinge and called Gerald an 'arrogant little pagan'.

Anne looked hard at me, then nodded slowly. 'I knew it!' she said. 'You've got toothache.'

She's getting me an emergency appointment for tomorrow!

TOMORROW, Lord! Please heal me before tomorrow! They don't work on Saturdays anyway, do they? Surely?

Saturday January 4th

I've been to the dentist!!! He's fixed my tooth!! What a wonderful, glowing, beautiful world this is!

Floated home to my stunning wife, my charming son, chatting happily as I walked, to God, who loves me so much!

Why on earth do people make such a fuss about going to the dentist? What's needed is a little courage, that's all.

Sunday January 5th

Took Anne tea in bed without getting grumpy.

Long quiet time.

Invited Richard Cook, Leonard Thynn and Edwin Burlesford, our elder, to Sunday tea. Gerald was on his best behaviour until near the end. He leaned forward and said very seriously, 'Richard, can I share a really amazing truth with you?'

Richard never learns.

'Yes?' he said—agog.

'Did you know,' said Gerald solemnly, 'that Gerald Coates can be rearranged to make "God's ale crate"?'

Anne looked concerned.

I choked in my tea.

Edwin laughed.

Leonard cackled.

Richard said, 'Who's Gerald Coates?'

Monday January 6th

Went into the Christian bookshop on my way home from work tonight.

All those books!

Gerald says Christian paperbacks are like Chinese meals. Very satisfying at the time, but it's not long before you want another one.

Bought a really great book about faith this time, though. It's called 'Goodness gracious—in God's name, what on Earth are we doing for Heaven's sake?'

A very witty title I feel.

It's all about how Christians should be able to move mountains by faith, if they are really tuned into God.

Very inspiring.

Waited 'till there was no-one around, then practised with a paper-clip. Put it on my desk and stared at it, willing it to move. Nothing! Tried commanding it in a loud voice.

Gerald came in just then, and said, 'What's all the shouting about, Dad?'

Could hardly tell him I was shouting orders at a paper-clip.

Said I was practising voice-projection.

He said, 'What for?'

I said, 'I don't know.' Felt really stupid.

Anne tells me someone is moving into the empty house next to us in the near future. Be nice if they were Christians, or, at least, easily convertible.

Tuesday January 7th

Gerald has managed to get himself a Saturday job at

one of the stores in town. He says it will help to pay for musical equipment for the band.

Anne said, 'Are you sure you won't be too tired after a week at college?'

Gerald laughed as though she'd said something really funny!

Had another go with the paper-clip tonight. I really took authority over it. Couldn't get it to budge.

Told God I'd give up anything he wanted, if he would just make it move half an inch.

Nothing!

All rather worrying really. If you only need faith the size of a mustard seed to move a mountain, what hope is there for me when I can't even get a paper-clip to do what it's told!

Wednesday January 8th

Richard and Edwin round for coffee this evening. We chatted for a while, then Gerald came in with an armful of leads and plugs and stuff.

Richard said, 'I hear you're going to be serving the Lord in Woolworth's on Saturday, Gerald'.

'That depends on whether he comes in or not,' said Gerald.

Funny thing—Richard, who eats, sleeps and breathes religion, looked awfully stern and disapproving when he heard this, but Edwin, who's an Elder and more or less in charge of our church, fell back in his chair with his feet in the air and laughed his head off. Odd!

Hoped Richard would leave before Edwin so that I could get some counselling re faith, but they left together.

Told Anne later that I'd heard about a man who tried to move a paper-clip by faith and couldn't do it. She yawned and said, 'Well, you always get your lunatic fringe, don't you?'

Thursday January 9th

Study-group tonight. We had a tape by Terry Virgo. Old Mrs Thynn said, 'Oh, yes, I've seen him on Pot Black. He takes off all them others, doesn't he?

Good prayer and worship time after that. Forgot about the paper-clip business for almost an hour, quite distracted by thinking about Jesus. Asked Gerald to get the numbers for drinks as the worship session ended.

He said, 'Right, you cuddly charismatics—hands down for coffee!'

I don't know how he gets away with it.

Rather odd couple here for the first time tonight. Mr and Mrs Flushpool. Said nothing all evening, just watched and listened. Edwin asked me quietly afterwards if I could ask them round for a meal one evening soon, as they'd just joined the church and didn't know anybody. Said I'd have to ask Anne about it. Edwin rushed off before I had a chance to put my faith problem to him.

Friday January 10th

Down to Unity Hall to see how the band's getting on. All that equipment! Sounded quite a bit better this time. Should think they've just about reached the stage where they could call themselves 'Not Particularly Good News For The Devil'.

They said that things like recording contracts were of no interest to them whatsoever, unless they were led in that direction, of course. William Farmer still seems somewhat over-vigorous to me. Someone's quite likely to stand up and exorcise him if he carries on like that in front of a few Christian audiences that I know.

Anne says the Flushpools can come on Thursday week. Didn't seem all that keen, though. Unusual for Anne. She's very hospitable usually.

Saturday January 11th

Got up early today to have a last go at that blasted paper-clip. Ended up hissing viciously at it, trying not to wake everybody up. When I gave up and opened the door, I found Anne and Gerald listening outside in their night-clothes, and looking quite anxious.

Anne said, 'Darling, why did you tell that paper-clip you'd straighten it out if it didn't soon get its damned act together?'

Explained with as much dignity as I could muster that I'd been conducting an experiment in faith, and had got a bit carried away when it didn't work.

Anne said, 'But, sweetheart, being a Christian isn't like joining the Magic Circle. Why would God want you to make a paper-clip move by faith?'

Gerald wiped his eyes and said, 'Dad, I think you're wonderful. I wouldn't swap you for anything.'

Rather liked him saying this. Anne did me a cooked breakfast. Felt quite happy really.

In Anne's bad books this evening. Had tea with Gerald when he came back from his first day at work, and asked him if there were any nice girls there. Developed into a discussion about women's looks.

Suddenly, Gerald said, 'When it comes down to it, I can't think of anyone who looks nicer than mum'.

Totally absorbed in the conversation, I said, 'Oh, *I* can!'

Anne put two more sausages on Gerald's plate, and took mine away before I'd quite finished.

Gerald can't have planned for that to happen . . . can he?

Sunday January 12th

Six-fruit-gum-talk on witnessing by Edwin this morning. Very good. Made you want to go straight out and witness to somebody. Drifted off into a pleasant day-dream in which I began to preach in the street and ended up with a huge crowd of people, all repenting in tears, and being healed of their sickness just by the touch of my hand. Very near to tears myself during the chorus that followed, as I pictured myself addressing vast assemblies of needy people throughout the world.

Came to with a shock as I realised that Edwin was asking for people to volunteer to do some actual street evangelism next Friday.

Sat as low down in my seat as I could, trying to look like someone whose earnest desire to evangelise has been thwarted by a previous appointment.

Leonard Thynn, sitting next to me, started poking his elbow in my ribs and whispering, 'Go on, you'll be good at it! I will if you will'.

Honestly! It's nothing like this in the books. Thynn made it seem as if we were two girl-guides volunteering to share a tent.

Put my hand up, so did Leonard. In a special meeting afterwards, Edwin said we would go out in pairs. Leonard and I have got to talk to people going in and out of the fish and chip shop in the High Street.

Feel a bit depressed at the prospect. Supposing I meet someone I know! Very fond of Leonard, but he's not the most reliable person in the world.

Asked Anne and Gerald what they thought about it tonight. Anne very supportive and encouraging. Gerald said that in his view, haddock eaters would prove to be less open than other customers in the fish shop. Tried to stop myself asking why, but cracked after about two minutes.

I said, 'Why should haddock eaters be less open?'

'Because,' said Gerald, 'they don't believe in cod'.

He must lie awake thinking these things up!

Monday January 13th

Lay awake myself for a while last night worrying

about Friday. I won't know what to say! Wish I was a frog-worshipper.

Found a note from Gerald on the breakfast table, suggesting that when I go out to change the world at the end of the week, I should bear in mind the important fact that Billy Graham is an anagram of 'Big rally ham'.

Richard phoned at lunchtime to ask if he could come round tomorrow evening with his son Charles to talk about a 'little problem'.

Rather puzzling. I thought Charles had already gone off for his second term at Bible School. All last term he wrote a letter a week back to the church, from which Edwin read occasional snippets. Gerald, who's seen the originals, says they make St Paul's epistles look like pagan telegrams.

Wonder what's gone wrong?

Tuesday January 14th

Went into the Christian bookshop again today, to see if they'd got anything good on street evangelism. Asked the man behind the counter eventually. There must be a special college somewhere, where they train Youth Hostel wardens, Lost Property officials and people who work in Christian bookshops.

I said, 'Have you got anything on street evangelism, please?'

'Street evangelism?' he said, with such annoyance and incredulity that I took an involuntary step backward, knocking over a life-size cardboard cut-out of Cliff Richard.

Panicked a bit. I said, 'Don't worry, it'll only take a second to resurrect him'. Picked Cliff up, then turned back towards the shop man who was breathing heavily through his nose.

'Yes,' I said, 'street evangelism—please'.

Came away eventually with what looks like a really great book, grudgingly excavated by the shopkeeper from the Christian Gardening section, where some frightened customer must have thrust it in his hurry to escape.

It's called 'Prayers, Principles, Practices and Probable Problems for Precinct Preachers' written by a man called A. P. Lunchington, who is, apparently, known affectionately in his part of the country as 'Lamp-post' Lunchington, owing to his untiring efforts to spread light on the pavements of his home town. I shall read it tomorrow when Richard's gone.

Richard arrived at 7.30 with Charles. Poor Charles looked a bit crazed, I thought. I said 'I thought your term started this week, Charles. Have you not been well?'

Charles said, 'The Lord has told me I'm not to go back to college. He would have me serve him elsewhere'.

Anne said, 'Where do you think he wants you to go, Charles?'

Charles said that he thought he should pack his bags and set out for the Near East as soon as possible, because God had made it clear that that was where he wanted him.

Anne said gently, 'How has he made it clear Charles?'

Charles leaned forward and spoke eagerly. 'It's amazing! Just about every time I open the Bible, there's something about Israel, or the Jews!'

Nearly laughed out loud, but Anne caught my eye. Richard looked unhappy.

Anne said, 'Charles, dear, what's going wrong at college?'

Had that feeling I sometimes have with Anne that I'd missed a whole chunk of conversation somewhere along the line. He hadn't mentioned a problem at college!

After a few tears from Charles and some more talk, it turned out that the poor old chap had felt lonely and useless and sinful all last term, and couldn't face going back for another three months of misery.

After a bit of prayer, lots of cake, and good advice from Anne, Charles said he thought he would go back after all.

Richard very pleased. Actually smiled! How did Anne know? Why didn't he talk to his own mother? I don't seem to understand anything!

Too late to start my new book tonight. Lay awake yet again, worrying about Friday. What shall I say, God? I don't know *anything*. What shall I say? What shall I say?

Wednesday January 15th

Sat down with Lunchington's book this evening, hoping to pick up a few good tips. What an amazing book! I don't know how the man finds time to eat or sleep. His life is literally one long succession of extraordinary miracles. Everyone he meets and everything he does could have come straight out of the New Testament. In fact the New Testament seems like an early and rather poor rehearsal for Lunchington's life.

The man doesn't know what it is to experience doubt or depression or failure or discouragement. Everyone he meets seems to get converted, and absolutely nothing gets him down. As for street evangelism—well! Lunchington has only to step out of his front door as far as I can see and instantly a hitherto deserted stretch of pavement will be thronged by a huge crowd, all jostling and shoving to get near enough to Lunchington to seek his help in making a commitment. Fell back in my chair exhausted at the end of the book.

Puzzled to find in the back of my mind a small but definite desire had arisen to kick Lunchington very hard, just between miracles. Dismissed this unworthy impulse as yet another ploy of the enemy, and dialled Leonard's number.

I said, 'Hello Leonard, I just wanted to tell you that I've been reading a really great book about witnessing, and I think we ought to do what this man does, and step out in faith on Friday night, dressed in our spiritual armour and know that the victory's won before we even begin!'

Thynn said, 'Oh, I agree, but can we pop into the George and have a jar or two on the way, just for a bit of Dutch courage, like?'

When I write *my* spiritual autobiography, Thynn will not be in it, except perhaps in a smartened-up form. Instead of suggesting 'a jar or two' he will say 'Amen, brother! Hallelujah!'

Thursday January 16th

Finished work early today. Took a walk out to the Mugley estate to visit Bill and Kitty Dove, our favourite old couple in the church. Found them eating crumpets and drinking tea by the fire. Bill and Kitty both smile as though a light's been switched on behind their faces.

Kitty said, 'Oooh, hurry up! Your crumpets'll get cold!'

Bill said, 'Here's a lovely cuppa. Get by the fire and tell us what that young Gerald's been up to'.

'Hee-hee-hee!' giggled Kitty. 'Young Gerald, hee-hee-hee!'

Told them about Christmas and Aunt Marjorie and Uncle Ralph and the band. They nodded and twinkled and nodded.

Bill said, 'What about you then?. What've you been up to?'

Told them about the witnessing on Friday.

Kitty beamed at me. She said, 'Oh, you are a lovely man to want to tell folks about our dear Jesus. Oh, he will be pleased!'

Suddenly felt weepy and soft. I said, 'It's not quite like that. I'm not a lovely man at all. . . '

Bill said, 'Oh, yes you are! God loves you fit to bust. He's crackers about you, so you must be lovely! Have another crumpet and don't be so daft!'

Left the Doves', feeling well fed.

Good study-group tonight, except when Doreen Cook said, 'Just for prayer, and strictly in confidence, but have you heard about Raymond?', and Edwin told her off gently for gossiping.

That couple, the Flushpools, were here again tonight. Said nothing at all, except when Gerald offered Mrs Flushpool a cup of coffee, and she said, 'I used to in the natural, but not any more'.

Asked Anne later why she'd been so funny about inviting them round. She just shook her head slowly and said she didn't know. Strange. . . .

Wish I knew what Doreen was going to say about Raymond.

Friday January 17th

Silly, sweaty quiet-time. Started by asking God for a sign that it would go alright this evening. Then remembered that bit about, '. . . it's a wicked generation that seeks a sign' and felt guilty. Then remembered John the Baptist losing his confidence in prison, and felt alright again, then remembered about Doubting Thomas and felt guilty again, then remembered Gideon's fleece and felt alright again.

Might have gone on like this forever, but Anne called out that it was time for work.

Gerald had left me a tiny silver cross to wear, and a note saying that witnessing is an anagram of 'sing in stew'.

Too nervous to eat before going out this evening. Spent a little while looking for a Bible that could have been 'The Guns of Navarone' for all anyone else knew. Found a smallish one eventually.

Leonard arrived at seven, clutching a huge brass-clasped family bible under his arm. Said his mother wanted him to bring it because *her* grandfather had used it to preach in the street in 1906. Thynn was dressed in a peculiar, old-fashioned, black suit, that looked as if it had once been used by an undertaker. Said it was his *best* suit.

Took up our position outside the fish-and-chip shop. Leonard looked like a severely deranged religious maniac out for the evening with his keeper. Felt really miserable and hopeless. Every time I *did* say something to one of the people going in and out of the shop, Leonard just echoed everything I said.

Me: Evening!
Customer: Evening!

Leonard:	Evening!
Me:	Still chilly, eh?
Customer:	(Laughing) Cor, yes!
Leonard:	Still chilly, eh?
Customer:	Pardon?
Leonard:	Still chilly, eh?
Customer:	(Uneasily) Err . . . yeh! (Departs hurriedly)

or

Me:	Excuse me.
Customer:	Yes, what . . . ?
Leonard:	(Paralysed with nerves) Excuse me.
Customer:	Pardon?
Leonard:	Err . . . excuse both of us.
Customer:	(Looking at Thynn's ridiculous suit and Bible) Yes, of course. You're excused. (Departs hurriedly)

Not the most dynamic religious exchanges of our time! In the end we both got hungry and went to buy some chips. Got talking without really trying, to a man called Ted who'd decided to eat his fish and chips in the warm before walking home. After we'd talked for a bit, Leonard, suddenly realising that this could be 'IT', started mouthing silently and intensely at me from behind Ted's shoulder, 'Go on, convert him!' Felt completely paralysed by this. Managed stumblingly to ask Ted if he'd ever thought that Christian values should be emphasised more strongly in society. Had quite a good discussion after that, ending, believe it or not, with Ted saying he wouldn't mind coming along to our church on Sunday morning!!

As we parted outside the shop, Ted said, 'Talking

about values in society an' all that, that's why I come down 'ere for my supper on Fridays now. There's a gang of yobs makes an 'orrible noise with their so-called music every Friday night for about two hours in that Unity 'all next door to us. Now *there's* somethin' that needs stoppin'! Anyway, see you Sunday mornin'. Goodnight.'

Later, after Leonard had gone home, singing 'We got one, we got one . . .' to the tune of Loch Lomond, I made sure Gerald wasn't around, and told Anne what Ted had said about the 'orrible noise.

'What's going to happen on Sunday,' I said, 'when Ted finds out that the gang of yobs who drive him out every Friday night are playing at our church? And that one of the leading yobs is *my son!*'

Anne said, 'I don't know what'll happen, but I'm sure it'll be alright. Remember Lunchington. He wouldn't worry.'

Huh! Lunchington! I dare say he would've brought all the fried fish back to life and given them a tract each.

Just said one prayer tonight. 'God, please save Ted. Amen.'

Saturday January 18th

Spent almost half an hour in the bathroom this morning, flattening down two tufts of hair which kept sticking up whatever I did, and making me look like the devil. Finally subdued them, only to have my hair ruffled violently by Gerald from behind as I was about to crack my egg.

Talk about full of beans! He said, 'Tomorrow's the day, Dad! Edwin came to listen last night and he said it's all systems go for Sunday morning. Mum, Dad.'

He was suddenly serious. 'You're going to be proud of me tomorrow.'

Anne said, 'I'm sure we are, dear.'

Opened my mouth, but my thoughts were strangling each other and no sound came out. Gerald didn't notice. He said, 'Must go, must go! Time for work! Fancy them being foolish enough to employ *me!*' Waltzed off through the door singing, 'Thats the blunder of Woolworth's . . .'

Disappeared, then put his head round the door a few seconds later.

'By the way, Dad.'

'Yes.'

'This chap you met last night.'

'Yes?'

'Well, our music might be the thing that brings him to a point where he makes a real decision.'

'Yes, Gerald,' I said. 'You could well be right.'

Hmmm. . . .

Saw our future neighbour briefly through the hall window this afternoon, going in to do some measuring or something, I expect. He looks relaxed, contented, smokes a big comfortable-looking pipe, there's a sort of glow of happiness around him. Unlikely to be a Christian, I would think. We shall find out when he moves in.

Sunday January 19th

Gerald up and out early to help get the band set up in the church. Very excited of course.

Arrived at the church with Anne later, half hoping that Ted wouldn't turn up. Sat at the back as usual and watched the door. Suddenly saw Ted hovering rather nervously in the doorway. Felt a sudden surge

33

of pride. That was my very own potential convert standing over there. Mine! Not anyone else's. Mine! Rose to my feet, intending to greet him with impressive, quiet modesty and warmth, when to my disgust, Thynn called out in a very loud voice, 'Ah, Ted, my old friend! When we asked you to come along to church the other evening, we weren't sure if you'd come or not. But here you are! Nothing to do with us of course. We all know that. Ha, ha!'

An outrageous exhibition to my way of thinking, and very frustrating. Could hardly stand up and say, 'Excuse me, everybody, but I was there as well. Actually, I did most of the talking.'

Leonard did at least bring him over to the empty chair that I'd saved next to me. Service began soon afterwards, led by Edwin himself, thank goodness. Edwin may stretch the old mesages out a bit at times, but he doesn't mind if you sit or stand or wave your hands in the air, or dance, or don't dance, or mime the whole of Goldilocks and the Three Bears, or whatever you like as long as what you do makes you feel comfortable, and doesn't interfere with anyone else. Ted seemed to quite enjoy the singing and the prayers. Edwin's message (5 wholly consumed fruit-gums and one unwrapped and halfway to the mouth) was a little disappointing. It was all about the Christian family and how we might get on better with each other, not the straight-down-the-line gospel message that I wanted Ted to hear. Kept looking sideways at him to see if there were tears in his eyes. Always a promising sign I feel. Not so much as a glisten as far as I could see, but he was certainly listening.

Then came the bit I dreaded. Edwin said, 'Now, everybody, I want you to listen to a brand new

Christian band, made up entirely of young people from the church. They've been practising really hard for today. They're going to play one of their own compositions—'Peace Will Come'. How about a nice encouraging round of applause for 'Bad News For The Devil!'

They *were* better, no doubt about that, but it was still pretty much a solid wall of noise, and young William Farmer drummed and sang like someone who'd got electric leads attached to some very vulnerable part of his body.

Noticed, rather nervously, that Ted was leaning forward in his chair with a puzzled expression on his face, listening intently to the music.

When it finished there was a stunned silence for a few moments, broken by old Mrs Thynn who said, 'What did 'e say they were called?'

Leonard said, 'Bad News For The Devil, mother.'

Hope for Gerald's sake, that the clapping which started just at that moment, obscured Mrs Thynn's reply of, 'Bad news for anyone, if you ask me.' Suddenly realised Ted was tapping me on the shoulder. ''Ere,' he whispered, 'this lot sounds just like the other lot down Unity 'all of a Friday.'

Cleared my throat, 'Actually, Ted, this lot *is* that lot, if you see what I mean. In fact, the one playing the lead guitar is my son—Gerald.'

'You mean,' said Ted, 'that when you asked me to come 'ere, an' afterwards I said about the yobs at . . . an' you still asked me?'

Suddenly realised Gerald had stepped forward to the microphone. All flushed and nervous, not like Gerald at all. Suddenly remembered him as a little boy.

'We're still pretty awful,' he said, 'but we're going to

35

get better, and I just wanted to say that song we just did, is—well, it's dedicated to a new friend of dad's called Ted, who's sitting over there at the back, and we just want to tell Ted that we hope he—he—well, becomes one of the family soon.'

Couldn't swallow for some reason. Ted was frowning and shaking his head slowly. 'Ain't never 'ad a family,' he said fiercely.

When the service ended Ted said, 'I want a word with the bloke in charge.' I introduced him to Edwin. Couldn't help just hinting that I'd invited him. They went off together into one of the side rooms.

Floated home.

I AM A CHRISTIAN WHO WITNESSES AND BRINGS PEOPLE TO THE LORD!!!

If things go on like this, I could end up being asked to speak at Christian conferences!

Monday January 20th

Woke up this morning feeling older, sterner, more patriarchal, somehow. Hoped Anne and Gerald would respond with more respect than usual to the aura of calm holiness that I sensed was all around me. When I came downstairs, Anne said, 'The cat's been sick behind the settee. Will you clear it up? I've got important things to do.'

Gerald handed me a folded piece of paper before setting off for college. When I opened it up I found a note saying, 'Dear Dad, did you know that "Inflated ego" is an anagram of "Feel a tin god"?'

Went to work.

Tuesday January 21st

Stopped on the way home this afternoon to chat to a man working in his garden just down the road from us. Thought I'd try out my new gift of witnessing. When I said I was a Christian, he said, 'Well, in that case, why don't you cut your ----ing hedge back a bit, so that we pagans don't have to step into the gutter every time we walk past your house?'

Walked on with flaming cheeks. What a horrible man! Needn't think he can tell *me* what to do and when to do it! Coincidentally, I *did* decide to have a go at the hedge today, but NOT because of what he said. Borrowed an electric trimmer from Mr Brain, our elderly neighbour, who comes to church sometimes, and did it in no time.

Didn't mention to Anne what the man said. She has gone on a bit about the hedge—since last summer in fact.

Gerald tells me he *will* be in when the Flushpools come tomorrow. Says he's curious.

Wednesday January 22nd

Phone call from Kitty Dove at work today. Says that Ted came to tea at their house yesterday, and said he wanted very much to follow Jesus, but Edwin had told him to think very carefully about it for a couple of weeks, and in the meantime, spend some time with the Doves.

'He speaks so highly of you, dear' said Kitty, 'and I think he's quite right!'

Why is it that when the Doves say nice things to me, I *really* want them to know I'm not as good as they think?

'He's asked if he can come and see us for the next two Friday evenings,' went on Kitty. 'Very particular about that, he was. Said Friday would be the best night for him if we didn't mind. Isn't that lovely?'

Smiled to myself. 'Yes,' I said, 'it is lovely.'

Gerald answered the phone at six o'clock this evening. Came back looking mystified.

He said, 'That was Mrs Flushpool. They can't come, she says her husband's laid up with an old disease that still affects him in the natural, and they'd like to come next Thursday, God willing, if that's alright. Can you 'phone back if it isn't?'

Isn't it WONDERFUL when something that *was* going to happen even though you didn't really *want* it to happen but you thought it *ought* to happen because it was right, doesn't happen after all, and it's *not* your fault?

Spent a very cosy evening with Anne and a bottle of wine. Gerald ate his own, Mr Flushpool's and Mrs Flushpool's share of the food, then went out for the evening. All very satisfactory.

I'd *love* to know what Doreen was going to say about Raymond last week. For prayer I mean. . . .

Thursday January 23rd

I keep thinking about the man down the road. I wish I hadn't cut the hedge now. Bet he smiles smugly every time he walks past our house. He thinks I've cut the hedge because of what he said. Huh! That's all he knows. If I wasn't feeling Christian forgiveness and goodwill towards him, I'd like to kneel on his chest and make him eat the hedge clippings.

No wonder St Paul says we mustn't be yoked with

unbelievers. He was obviously thinking of people like this man, who doesn't understand things like love and peace and Christian charity.

Not that it bothers me. Why should it? I feel that the Lord is saying I mustn't make contact with him again, so I won't. So that's that! I won't give it another thought. Not another thought.

Study group at someone else's house tonight. Didn't go. Felt rather ill and down. Anne and Gerald came back very happy and nauseatingly healthy. Perked up a little later on when Gerald told me that Mrs Thynn described tonight how her grandmother had not been able to afford to pay for her father's funeral, but the Lord had 'wonderfully undertaken'.

Friday January 24th

Had an awful nightmare last night. Really bad! It all happened in church. I was standing up at the front behind a barber's chair and somehow I knew that I'd just finished shaving all the members of the congregation, men, women *and* children. I was the only unshaven person there. In fact, my beard, which was bright green for some reason, came down way below my knees.

Suddenly (in my dream) the doors at the back crashed open and the man down the road stormed in, pointed an accusing finger at me, and shouted, 'He shaved others! Himself he could not shave!'

Woke up sweating and trembling. Had to reach out and touch Anne's shoulder to make sure everything was alright.

Stupid, meaningless dream!

Still feeling grotty. Anne wouldn't let me go to work today. Just a mild spot of 'flu I expect. Prayed for healing but wasn't. Why don't people like Lunchington put that sort of thing in their books?

When Anne came up to bring me a hot drink and my favourite creamed mushrooms on toast, I waited 'til she'd tidied the bed and stopped fussing round me, then I said, 'Anne, just tell me one solitary thing that shows God cares about me being ill.'

She said, 'He's provided you with a full-time nurse who doesn't ask to be paid, and loves you very much. Will that do for a start?'

Thinking to brighten up Anne's day with a little joke, I replied, 'Great! When does she arrive?'

Had to have a slight relapse later to make Anne sympathetic again.

Saturday January 25th

Felt a little better this morning. Two visitors while Anne was out. Richard came round to say that he'd had a 'picture'. Why don't I ever have pictures? He wondered if his picture might be connected with my illness.

He said, 'I saw, as it were, a dartboard, and, impaled upon the dartboard by means of a dagger, was a small jellyfish, and, as I watched, it was revealed to me that the creature's name was Stewart.'

I shall never understand why Richard says these things in front of Gerald. Gerald nodded gravely, and said, 'Well, there you are dad. That's it. It's "The Revenge of the Jellyfish", like in the horror films. Obviously at some time in your life you must have stepped on one called Stewart while you were paddling, and now they've found a way to get their own back by giving you the 'flu.'

40

Richard said, 'That doesn't explain the dartboard.'

I said, 'Isn't it time for you to go to work, Gerald?'

Thanked Richard for sharing his picture with me. Said I couldn't see an obvious connection, but I'd bear it in mind.

Next visitor was Edwin with some mint imperials, which I love, and the offer of a chat. Started to tell him about Richard's picture, but he stopped me and said, 'Don't tell me the details. Dear old Richard means well, but he does get a bit carried away sometimes. The thing about these "pictures" is that every now and then you get one that really is from God. You just have to think them through, pray about them, and decide calmly for yourself.'

Did all that later. Didn't take long. Jellyfish! Really!

Just before dozing off this afternoon, I said to Anne, 'You know that man down the road who looks like a jellyfish?'

'No,' said Anne.

'Well, he's fattish and—well, fattish.'

'No.'

'Roses in the front.'

'Oh, yes,—fattish, yes.'

'You don't know his name, do you?'

'No.'

'You don't know if he's called Stewart?'

'No.'

'Oh.'

'Why?'

'Nothing . . . it doesn't matter.'

Sunday January 26th

Much better, but decided to stay in today so as to

be fit for work tomorrow. Gerald left me some of the band's song lyrics to read while he and Anne were at church. Had a look at the one they did on Sunday last. 'Peace Will Come'. I am copying the words into my diary. There are two verses.

Verse I   Peace will come,
Peace will come,
Peace will come,
Peace will come,
Peace will come,
Peace will come,
Peace will come,
Peace will come,
Peace will come,
Peace will come,
Peace will come,
Peace will come,
What will come?
Peace will come.

Verse II   Peace has come,
Peace has come,
Peace has come,
Peace has come,
Peace has come,
Peace has come,
Peace has come,
Peace has come,
Peace has come,
Peace has come,
Peace has come,
Peace has come,
What has come?
Peace has come.

(Repeat verses I and II three times)

Gerald said they spent hours polishing up the lyrics on this one! Seems a bit of a waste of time to me. By the time *any* words have fought their way out between William Farmer's tonsils they could sound like anything at all. Still, Gerald's keen. Mustn't be discouraging.

Monday January 27th

Quite well again. Went to work. Have decided to walk *up* the road and through the cemetery every morning from now on. It's a bit longer, but the exercise will do me good.

Just as I left Anne said, 'Oh, by the way, what about him?'

Pretended not to know what she was talking about.

She said, 'You know, you were rambling on about him in bed on Saturday afternoon. Something about jellyfish, and was he called Stewart? The man down the road—with the roses. What about him?'

Panicked. I said, 'Oh, yes, I remember now. I—I saw him in his garden one day, and thought I'd like to —to write a poem about him. It's not finished yet.'

Anne said, 'You're writing a poem about the man down the road?'

'Yes.'

'The man you think looks like a jellyfish, and might be called Stewart?'

'Err . . . yes. There's err . . . a dartboard in it too. Anyway, I must go, Anne. I'll be late for work.'

Left Anne silently mouthing 'dartboard' to herself. I'd only got a few yards up the road when she called me from an upstairs window.

'Darling, that's not the way to work! I know you

haven't been for three days, but you can't have forgotten already.'

Tried to call back casually. 'Oh, it's okay. I know it's a bit longer, but it'll do me good.'

Anne said, 'Darling, it's nearly a *mile* longer, and you're late already. What *are* you talking about?'

Felt like screaming! I said firmly, 'Anne, I feel led to go this way, and go this way I shall!'

Late for work. Felt guilty and confused all day. Worn out by walking the long way home this evening. Feel like killing somebody! The man down the road for instance.

Anne kept looking at me as if I was a loony.

Just after switching the light off tonight, she said, 'Have you finished your poem yet, darling?'

Foolishly replied, 'Yes.'

Anne said, 'Oh, good. You must read it to me in the morning.'

Waited till she was asleep, then crawled out of bed to write the damned thing! What am I going to do if Gerald's there when I read it? He knows all about Richard's 'picture'. What a stupid mess! Hope Armageddon's scheduled for tonight.

Tuesday January 28th

Woke with a headache.

At breakfast Anne said, 'Can I hear your poem now, darling?'

Gerald said, 'Poem? Has *dad* written a poem?'

Said it as though he'd just heard about a pig who'd been taught to dance Swan Lake. *He* can talk. 'Peace will come'. Huh!

I said, 'Yes, Gerald, I've written a poem.'

Anne said, 'Your father is very struck by a man

down the road, Gerald. That's what the poem is about. Go on, darling. Read it to us.'

Anne turned away for a moment just then, so I was able to look pleadingly at Gerald and put my finger to my lips. He looked intrigued but co-operative. Read the poem out.

Oh, man down the road,
You with the roses,
And a face like a dartboard,
Were you fathered by a jellyfish?
Or what?
You, whose name may not be Stewart,
How I'd love to watch Eric Bristow,
Practise on you.
Or anybody really.

Looked at my wife and son as I finished, and realised that once again, they are, quite reasonably, convinced that I am going round the bend.

Came home tonight (the long way) to find that Ted had phoned earlier. Could I phone back? Rather pleased really. Reflected, as I dialled the number, that Ted probably sees me as a sort of spiritual giant, silly, but quite understandable.

When I got through he said, 'Oh, good stuff! Thing is, there's this bloke at work 'oo might be interested in—well, you know, God an' that. Kitty Dove said why not bring 'im round to see you, 'specially as 'e lives in the same road as you. Watcha think?'

I said, 'What's his name?'

'Simmonds,' said Ted.

'No, no, I mean his first name. Is he called Stewart?'

Ted sounded puzzled. 'No 'e's called Norman. But

listen. Can I bring 'im round tomorrow evenin' at about seven o'clock?'

'Yes Ted,' I replied. 'Yes. Please do bring him round. See you tomorrow. 'Bye.'

His name may be Norman, but something tells me that, without any doubt at all, the chap coming to my house with Ted tomorrow night, is the chap who told me to get my ----ing hedge cut.

Wednesday January 29th

8.00 a.m.

Woke up in deep gloom. A near-fatal road accident would just about hit the spot as far as I'm concerned today. Don't want to actually die, just be severely—and painlessly—injured, enough to distract everybody from this lunatic fever-dream of hedge-cutting and dartboards and walking the long way to work and the man down the road being interested in God.

Wish the J.W.s had got to him first. No I don't. Yes I do. No I don't. Oh-BISCUITS!

This may be the last entry in my diary. I'm setting off for work now, and I'm a troubled, dangerous man. I may *never* come back!

6.00 p.m.

Back at the usual time. Slightly cheered by a phone-call at work from Bill Dove.

He said, 'Hello, mate! Got time for a chat with an old sinner?'

'Yes, Bill,' I said gloomily, 'if you've got time for a chat with a middle-aged idiot.'

Bill chuckled. 'I know, I know,' he said. 'You've got yourself in a real pickle, haven't you?'

'*How* do you know, Bill?'

Another chuckle. 'Just know, don't I? Now listen! It's all planned out—got that? It's *all* planned out.'

'Planned out?'

'Certainly. Now, I want you to call me tonight, late, and say either "Bill, you're a silly old fool, and I'm never going to listen to you again," or—"Hello Bill, God's in charge." Got that? Good! See yer.'

Midnight: Ted and the Simmonds man arrived at seven o'clock precisely. We all sat stiffly around the sitting room waiting for someone to say something. Everyone seemed to be staring at *me*.

I could feel a sort of mad laugh bubbling up in me, when the doorbell rang suddenly and broke the tension. Anne answered it, and came back a second or two later with our new pipe-smoking neighbour, who smiled round at everybody without any self-consciousness, and introduced himself as Frank Braddock.

'Moved in today,' he announced easily. 'Thought I'd stroll over and say hello to my new neighbours. Anyone mind if I smoke?'

Looked intently at me suddenly.

'Now, your name is . . . ?'

'Adrian,' I said rather feebly. 'That's my name.'

'Ah! Adrian is it? Right!'

He pointed his pipe-stem at me.

'You know . . .' he smiled richly, 'you're the only man I've ever seen cutting his hedge in near-darkness in the middle of winter as if his life depended on it. And I said to myself that day—I said 'When I move in I'm going to *ask* that man *why* he was doing that. So—why were you?'

Braddock plumped down into an easy chair and began filling his pipe with calm enjoyment.

Never felt so embarrassed in my life.

Looked down at the carpet to hide my burning face. Thought how much Simmonds must be enjoying this moment. Suddenly thought—what the heck? I'll tell 'em all what happened, they can all have a jolly good laugh, then they can do what they like. Looked up, and was about to speak, when I noticed to my surprise that Simmonds, who only has hair on the sides of his head, was also one big blush.

'Actually,' he stumbled, 'I was hoping that wouldn't get brought up tonight . . .'

'What on earth do you mean?' said Anne.

'Well . . .' Simmonds cleared his throat, 'You see, I'd had the mother-and-father of a row with the wife that day, and when you came along . . .'—he pointed at me—'. . . and started talking about being a Christian, well—I just blew my top and gave you all the aggro that I'd piled up ready for the wife. The first thing I thought of was your hedge, 'cause I walk past it to work every day, and it *did* stick out a bit, but not much. But then . . . !'

He leaned forward, very animated.

'Instead of giving me a mouthful back, like I deserved, you went off and started cutting the hedge! And I thought that was—well, I thought you must be quite—well—I dunno—quite unusual.'

His blush deepened.

'Anyway, I lost my nerve after that. You won't believe this, but I even started walking the other way to work so I didn't have to go past your house and run the risk of seeing you.' He laughed ruefully. 'That's the kind of idiot I am, I'm afraid.'

Caught Anne's eye and looked away hastily.

'And then,' Norman resumed, 'old Ted here told me he'd got interested in what was going on up at the church, and I thought I'd like to find out what it was all about, so he suggested coming along here tonight. Well . . . when I saw which house it was when we got here just now, I nearly did a bunk! But then I remembered the way you went off and did that hedge and I thought, Oh, well, in for a penny, in for a pound, so here I am.'

He leaned back, obviously glad to have got it off his chest. I looked round. Ted was staring at me as if I was a modern-day St Francis. Anne looked like someone who's just finished a difficult jigsaw puzzle. Gerald's face was in his hands, but his shoulders were gently shaking. As for Frank Braddock, he was leaning forward, elbows on his knees, pipe clenched between his teeth, gazing fixedly at me with a funny little expectant smile lighting up his eyes.

I said, 'Norman, you're all wrong about me. I cut the hedge because I was embarrassed, and I wanted to make you eat the clippings to get back at you for making me feel stupid. And . . . (A difficult one this) . . . I walked a different way to work as well, and I told Anne that—that it was because I felt led to go that way, and—and, oh, Lord . . . !'

All got sorted out after that. A lot of laughter and chat. Braddock didn't stay much longer. Saw him to the door. Just before closing the door, I said, 'Frank —can I ask you, are *you* a Christian?'

He raised a bushy eyebrow. 'Guess!'

Didn't know what to say. What an embarrassing question! Still don't know the answer. When I didn't say anything, he just clapped me on the shoulder and strode off down the path, shouting 'Goodnight mate!' as he went. Strange man!

After they'd all gone, Anne hugged me and made a cup of tea. 'Darling,' she said, 'why let things get so complicated?'

Gerald said, 'Come off it, mum! Dad wouldn't be dad if he didn't complicate things.'

Just about to follow Anne up to bed, when I remembered Bill Dove. Phoned him straightaway. I said, 'Bill, you're a silly old fool, and I'm never going to listen to you again.'

He chuckled, 'It went alright then?'

'Yes Bill,' I said, 'God's in charge.'

Thursday January 30th

Walked to work the *short* way this morning.

Suddenly felt oppressed by the prospect of the Flushpools' visit this evening. Would have been nice to just enjoy the uncomplicated atmosphere for once. Still, as a Christian, you're lumbered aren't you?

Came home to find Anne tired and tense after cleaning and baking and preparing the meal all day. Gerald breezed into the kitchen as we were enjoying a cup of tea, peered at a rather sad looking sponge on the side, and said, 'I see you've made a Bishop of Durham Cake, Mum.'

'What do you mean, Gerald?' said Anne, quietly but icily.

'All the right ingredients, but nothing's risen,' replied Gerald cheerily. Dodged the wet dish-cloth with ease. Slipped hastily out of the door before she could find more ammunition.

I said, 'You've got to laugh.'

Anne said, 'Have you?'

Flushpools arrived at about seven-thirty. We all sat down straightaway in the dining room. Mrs Flushpool, who looks like a collection of black plastic bags half-filled with water, glanced around and said,

'Dear Anne, such a problem keeping a room of this

size *really* clean. How we need the presence of the mighty one, even in our most intimate wifely duties.'

Mr Flushpool, who bears a remarkable resemblance to those old photographs of Crippen, said, in a deep tomb-like voice, 'Amen to that!'

From that point onwards, Anne said hardly anything. Mrs Flushpool described at great length how she had been converted from fleshly works and appetites since being washed in the blood, and how, in consequence, she was now able to turn her back on those things that she used to do in what she called 'the natural'. Everything she said seemed to have a sort of dampness about it. She and her husband refused wine, saying that Christians should be ashamed to have it in the house, as it led to carnal excess. At this point Mr Flushpool let out another sonorous 'Amen to that!' Coffee was also frowned on as something that was wont to stimulate inappropriately in the natural.

Gerald, with a perfectly straight face, asked Mrs Flushpool if she used to go swimming in the natural. She replied fervently that her bodily flesh would never again rouse any man to a fever of sensual lust.

Mr Flushpool opened his mouth very wide to say, 'Amen to that!' but thought twice and shut it.

Mrs Flushpool went on to talk, with gleaming eyes, about the dangers of the occult, becoming so vehement, that she started to froth slightly at the mouth, and had to use a red paper napkin.

Quite glad when they got up to go at about 10 o'clock. As she left, Mrs Flushpool said, 'Thank you so much for supper, *dear* Anne. You must come round to us soon, and have a *proper* meal.'

Through the closed door we heard a final 'Amen to that' as Mr Flushpool marched to his nightly fate.

I said to Anne, 'Well, what did you think?'

Rarely seen Anne look so grim. She said, 'They have a certain emetic quality. I'm going to bed—in the natural. Are you coming?'

'Yes,' I replied. 'Amen to that!'

Friday January 31st

Strolled down to Unity Hall again tonight to hear B.N.F.T.D. Gerald tells me that Elsie (flute) and William (vocal hysteria) are deeply in love with each other. Doesn't seem to have slowed him down at all. When he sings, the words still come out of him like rats from a burning building. He told me afterwards that if the Lord leads him into being an international rock star, he's prepared to be obedient, even if it means travelling all over the world and staying in expensive hotels, and earning huge amounts of money. The only drawback at the moment, he said, is that his father wants him to work in the family fruit shop in the High Street.

Said that if he's going to spend the rest of his life selling bananas and turnips to fat old ladies he might as well die right now.

Young Elsie, who was listening, flushed with sympathetic indignation, and said she would stand by William to the 'absolute death', and anyway, they both felt led to carry on and make Bad News For The Devil into one of the greatest Christian rock bands of all time.

Felt rather flattered being taken into their confidence until, on the way home, Gerald said, 'Sorry you had to listen to all that, Dad. They say the same thing to anyone who's stupid enough to stand and listen. They're just loopy about each other.'

Got my own back later on when, after much thought, I was able to announce that 'Gerald Plass' was an anagram of 'All pa's dregs'. Gerald gave me another of those 'pig dancing Swan Lake' looks. Think he was quite impressed really, though.

Anne says we ought to visit another of her Great aunts tomorrow, Aunt Felicity, who used to be married to a sailor. Suppose I'll have to go. Somehow I always end up feeling depressed after an encounter with this particular old lady. Oh, well, it probably won't be too bad. They say she's got very senile lately.

Saturday February 1st

Off in the car this morning to visit Aunt Felicity at the Eight Bells Home for Maritime Relicts. Anne went into the room first to explain quietly that we'd come to visit while I waited outside the open door.

Anne said, 'Hello, Auntie, it's Anne, your niece. I've come to see you. Adrian's here too—he's just outside the door.'

''E can't be,' replied Aunt Felicity in a shrill squawk, ''e's dead, thank gawd!'

'Now Auntie,' said Anne, 'you know you don't mean that really. Look, here he is now, come to visit you.'

Aunt Felicity sat up a little, inspected me closely with her beady little black eyes as I walked into the room, and then relaxed back onto her pillow, and squawked triumphantly, 'There you are! Told yer! I said 'e was dead!'

Felt a bit non-plussed. Leaned right over her and said in a loud voice, 'Auntie, it's me! Adrian! I'm alive!'

She stared up at me for a moment, then said dispassionately, 'You want to get 'im cremated, Anne love, 'fore 'e starts to smell.'

Gave up and said nothing for the rest of the visit. There's something deeply discouraging about being in the same room as someone who's convinced that you're a corpse.

Sunday February 2nd

Lay awake for some time last night, thinking about getting old like Auntie Felicity, and dying all alone in some nursing home. Wanted to wake Anne and Gerald up and do something like playing Monopoly —all cosy together. In the middle of the night I'd have gladly given up my glorious resurrection if we could just stay as we are. I don't want to die!'

If I'd known George Farmer was leading the service this morning I wouldn't have gone. He started by shouting things at the congregation in a loud, thirty-six-visions-before-breakfast sort of voice.

G.F.	Good morning!
Congr	(feebly) Morning . . .
G.F.	(Not satisfied) I said GOOD MORNING!!
Congr	(forcing slightly more volume out between tired tonsils) Good morning!
G.F.	Are we joyful?
Congr	(in a strangled bleat, like a herd of dyspeptic sheep) Ye-e-e-s
G.F.	Well we don't *sound* very joyful! I'll ask you again! ARE WE JOYFUL?
Congr	(Panicked into believing that lack of volume is a sin) Y-E-E-E-s!

54

G.F.	That's more like it! And are we glad to be in the House of God this morning?
Congr	(Playing the game well now) Y-E-E-E-S!!
G.F.	(Cupping his hand playfully round his ear) And where do we all hope to go one day?
Congr minus one	H-E-A-V-E-N!!
Thynn	T-E-N-E-R-I-F-E!! (Pause—all look at Thynn)
Thynn	Sorry—H-E-A-V-E-N!!

As a token of appreciation I passed Leonard my penultimate fruit-gum. Greater love hath no man . . .

Just before Anne went up to bed tonight, I said, 'You know all the business about death and going to heaven, and all that?'

'Yes,' said Anne, yawning loudly.

'Well—I'm completely confused about it.'

Anne smiled a very weary smile. 'Well there's one thing, darling. At least you're consistent.'

Was that a compliment? I've been sitting here for half an hour since Anne went up, and I'm still not sure.

It's good to be consistent—isn't it? Surely?

Monday February 3rd

I don't want to die.

Gerald invited Vernon Rawlings and William Farmer round this evening. They're all young. They don't even think about dying. All William Farmer thinks about is the band, and how badly he's getting on with his dad. It appears that George left him in charge of the shop for half an hour on Saturday, with clear instructions to write a big sign to go over the fruit and veg., out on the pavement. Unfortunately, William was so distracted by the sight of Elsie unpacking the water-melons that he left out a vital word, and when George came back he found a little crowd of people outside the shop all picking up fruit and squashing it in their hands. When George asked them what on earth they were doing, a fat little girl holding a plum in one fist and a peach in the other, nodded towards the sign that William had propped up against the shop window and said, ''S'alright—look!'

The sign said 'PLEASE DO SQUEEZE THE FRUIT'

William said that when his father stormed, wild eyed, into the back room, where he and Elsie were counting each other's fillings, and shouted, 'There's

no not in it! With no not it means do! Why the hell didn't you put a not in it?', he thought his dad had gone completely mad. It didn't help that Elsie, who is a very spirited, if rather foolhardy girl, put her hands on her hips, looked George straight in the eye, and said, 'Now's your chance to *prove* you're a Christian, Mr Farmer!'

Poor old George. I don't think I would have felt very Christian if someone had just crushed my fruit. Still, he was alright by Sunday morning. *He* seems to be looking forward to dying and going to heaven. Rang Richard Cook tonight and asked him what *he* was most looking forward to about going to heaven. He cleared his throat into religious gear and said, 'I am looking forward to being able to worship and adore the Lord for all eternity. What greater joy can there be than this?'

Well, of course I go along with that. I mean—yes, absolutely . . .

Tuesday February 4th

Still feeling gloomy about death. Keep looking round at all the old familiar people and things, then trying to imagine swapping them for something like one of our Sunday meetings only going on for ever, instead of an hour and a half. Gerald tried to cheer me up by pointing out that Ishmael is an anagram of 'I lash 'em!'

Nearly smiled.

Wednesday February 5th

Am I a Christian? Don't want to die.
Don't want to go to heaven. Certainly don't want

to go to hell. Asked Anne tonight if she thought I'd enjoy heaven. She said, 'Only if they give you your own special little corner to moan in.'

Charming! When have I ever moaned?

Thursday February 6th

Frank Braddock round tonight after study-group. Just appeared at the door, strode through to the sitting room, and collapsed in an armchair. Still don't know if he's a Christian, even after what happened next. The doorbell rang and Anne came in after a few seconds with Mrs Flushpool who said she'd discovered the loss of an intimate personal item after arriving home from the study-group, and as she wasn't sure how long it would be before Anne tidied up again, and she didn't want to put temptation in anyone's way, she thought she'd just pop back to see if it had slipped down behind a cushion. No sign of whatever unspeakable object she was looking for, so she turned her attention to Frank Braddock, sitting happily in a little cloud of sweet-smelling tobacco smoke. I introduced him.

'Well, Mr Braddock,' she said, lips pursed in diapproval 'and are you one of the elect?'

Braddock stared at her for a moment, rose slowly to his feet, and spoke with deep gravity and immense dignity.

'Madam,' he said, 'I am a member of the M.C.C..'

'And what, pray, is the M.C.C.?'

Braddock replied with deep reverence. 'The Marylebone Cricket Club, Madam.'

Momentarily taken aback, Mrs Flushpool rallied

her forces, gave the black plastic bags a little shake, and returned to the attack.

'And may I ask, Mr Braddock, how membership of this *club* will be of assistance to you when you stand before the judgement seat, and things of the natural are of no account?'

Braddock's gaze was unwavering.

'My M.C.C. membership card, madam, guarantees me, at any time, and at all times, admission to the Lords Enclosure.'

Mrs Flushpool tried hard to think of a reply to this, but it was clear that she was defeated, and she hadn't even *started* on the pipe! After murmuring something perfunctory, she was gone, leaving Anne hugging herself with satisfaction, and Frank puffing away calmly in the armchair.

As Frank left later, I said, 'You still haven't told me, you know. *Are* you a Christian?'

'Guess!' he said, just like last time.

Later I asked Anne if *she* thought he was a Christian. She laughed helplessly. 'You are a funny man,' she said. 'Of course he is!'

Friday February 7th

I don't want to die, despite the ludicrous evening I've just been through.

Elsie Burlesford rang me when I got home tonight. She said I'd been so understanding last week she thought I might agree to talk to William's father about his cruel treatment of his only son. Reminded Elsie that William has two brothers. 'Well, one of his only sons then,' she said.

Rather pleased to be asked really. Said I'd do what

I could. She said thanks, and could I not tell William she'd phoned, as he was very independent and brave, and wouldn't want help from anyone else.

Five minutes later William phoned to ask if I'd mind having a word with his dad about the band meeting tonight. Apparently George told him on Saturday that part of his punishment would be not going to B.N.F.T.D. practice for two weeks. Could I possibly change his mind, and would I mind not telling Elsie he'd phoned as she was very sensitive and mustn't be upset? Said I'd have a go. Felt a bit like Henry Kissinger.

Ten minutes later Gerald came crashing in to ask if I'd try to get William's dad to let him come to band practice this evening. Didn't wait for an answer. Just said 'Thanks, dad,' and rushed off again, then rushed back to ask if I could please not tell William or Elsie that he'd asked, because he knew they'd hate to think anyone was interfering. Rushed off again, shouting, 'Ta, dad! You're a real pal. See you later!'

The moment the door slammed the phone rang. It was Anne. She'd stopped off on her way to late shopping to ring me. She'd run into Elsie Burlesford a little earlier and heard about how upset William was. 'The poor little girl's in a terrible state about it all,' said Anne. 'George likes you. Can't you give him a ring and suggest a chat. Oh, and don't tell Elsie I told you. It was all strictly confidential. You know what Elsie's like! See you later, darling. Bye— love you!'

Felt a bit dazed as I put the phone down. Felt even more dazed when it rang *again*. It was Edwin, Elsie's father. Said that Elsie had just been expressing the view that George Farmer needed to be delivered from a spirit of intolerance and anger, and was Edwin, as her father, and the Elder of her church, prepared to 'see to it'.

'The thing is,' sighed Edwin, 'you know what old George is like. It's nothing to do with a spirit of anything. He's just a very passionate type, and, sometimes he goes over the top. After all young William was a *bit* careless. Anyway, what I was going to say was that George thinks a lot of you, so why don't you talk to him—cool him down a bit? Elsie's going to burst if something doesn't happen soon. She'll be up at the Farmer's with a wooden stake and a sprig of garlic before long. Oh, and, if you don't mind, keep this call to yourself, Elsie didn't want anyone but me to know how she felt. Is that okay?'

'Yes, but . . .'

'Super! See you on Sunday. Cheers!'

My only consolation as I put the phone down yet again, was that there was no-one else left to ring. Made the tatal mistake of getting into the bath. I'd just said, 'Aaaah!' as I sank back into the hot water, when the damned thing rang *again*. Went back down in a towel, determined to give short shrift to whichever member of the Elsie Burlesford fan club was on my back now. Sensitive indeed! From what I'd seen of Elsie she was about as sensitive as an avalanche. Picked up the phone.

'Ah! Hello, Adrian—hope I'm not interrupting anything.'

'Ah, George,' I said, 'I was going to ring you about . . .'

'Listen, brother!', boomed George. 'I need a favour from you. Y'see . . . well, fact is I got a bit snappy with young William the other day—little blighter forgot to put a not in it . . . anyway, in the heat of the moment I said he had to miss band practice for a couple of weeks, and—well, I guess I got a bit carried away really. Thing is, I want to let him off, but I don't want him to think I've gone soft. So . . .'

'Yes George?'

'So would you mind if I told him that you'd talked me into changing my mind. Would that be alright, brother? Would it?'

'Yes George, that's fine. You go ahead. Goodbye, George.'

Went back to my not quite hot enough bath and said to God, 'You *do* work in mysterious ways, don't you?'

Later, at Unity Hall, after William's usual impression of a man who's stubbed toes on both his feet, Elsie came up and gazed at me with wide admiring eyes.

'D'you know who you remind me of, Mr Plass, even to look at, a bit?'

Here we go, I thought, the old Henry Kissinger bit. Ah, well, a spot of hero-worship never did anyone any harm.

'Who's that then?' I asked.

'Claire Raynor,' said Elsie.

Saturday February 8th

Thought there might be something in the Christian bookshop about confusion. When I asked the shopkeeper, he said, 'Confusion?!' as though I'd asked for a bag of coal. Finally unearthed a tape cassette at the back of the Christian Plumbing shelf entitled 'Collected Correctional Courses for Confused Christians', by Doctor William Worplesdon, or 'Windolene Worplesdon' as he is commonly known.

Settled down this evening to listen. Really looking forward to some clear teaching about death and heaven and all the things I've been worrying about. This is how the tape began:

'My name is Worplesdon. Greetings to you, confused brother, or confused sister. My message divides into three sections, the first of which consists of two parts, Part "A" being approached from four perspectives, the most immediate of which can be sub-divided into two areas, the initial one breaking down into four main categories, beginning with a multi-faceted topic, the primary facet being contained under six main headings, and I would like to look at number one from two points of view, the first consisting of five components, the commencing item of which falls naturally into seven sections, starting with a three point introduction to part one of the opening item in the first stage of the primary point of a six-step argument on the subject of confusion in the church . . .'

Must have been the click of the cassette player switching itself off that woke me up. I dread to think what Worplesdon's like when he's speaking to people who *aren't* confused.

Dragged myself miserably upstairs to bed. Anne's asleep so I can't talk to her. Gerald's left a note on my pillow to say that Alvin Stardust is an anagram of 'I trust vandals', and now *he's* fast asleep.

There's just me—me and God.

Help me, God! I'm confused. . . .

Sunday February 9th

That monk who came at Christmas was in church again today. Edwin had asked him to do a question and answer session. Put my fruit-gums away unopened. Father John looked pale and tired, but I honestly thought they'd rigged a spotlight up at the back because there seemed to be a sort of shininess round his face as he sat quietly on a stool at the front.

Mrs Flushpool asked the first question.

She said, 'I find it strange, reverend—I cannot call you Father as I have scriptural reservations—that on your previous visit you barely mentioned the judgement of God on sin committed in the natural. Perhaps you do not feel sinful?'

Father John blinked. 'Oh, I'm a ratbag,' he declared, with enthusiasm, 'but I do feel so *very* forgiven. You see, God's crazy about me, just as he's crazy about you. Salvation was his idea you know—not ours.' He pointed at Mrs Flushpool. 'If you were to commit a foul sin with every person in your street, and then you said to God "I really am honestly and sincerely most awfully sorry," he would say, "Great! Let's start all over again." Marvellous, isn't it?'

Mrs Flushpool, presumably wrestling inwardly with the image of herself committing foul sins with every person in her street, splashed back down into her seat, looking rather breathless.

Leonard Thynn leaned across and whispered in my ear, 'He knows a different God to the one I do. His God's *nice*!'

Suddenly found myself on my feet. Felt about six years old as I spoke.

'I don't want to die . . .'

'No,' said Father John, 'neither do I. Life can be very good. I'm sure Jesus didn't want to die either. His friends and family, the natural world, laughter, tears, work—he loved it all I'm sure.'

'But heaven—the idea of heaven seems so . . . I don't know . . .'

'What is your name?' asked the monk.

'Adrian . . .'

'Adrian, what are you interested in—*really* interested in, I mean?'

'Cricket.' Didn't mean to tell the truth. It just slipped out.

'So,' said Father John, 'for you, Adrian, God has to make sure that heaven is at least as exciting and stimulating and satisfying as scoring a century against Australia at Lords. Is that your wife sitting next to you?'

Anne smiled and nodded.

'If Adrian keels over suddenly, my dear, and he's on the point of death, you'll know what to do now?'

'Yes,' laughed Anne, 'I'll buckle a pair of pads on him—quick.'

Felt as if someone had opened a window and let air into a stuffy room. Went home for a very enjoyable lunch. I invited Leonard who brought *three* bottles of wine! Anne and I, knowing poor old Leonard's problems in this area, drank as much of it as we could before he could get his hands on it. Leonard stayed sober, Anne seemed unaffected, but I ended up in the same position as the football team that Gerald supports—struggling at the foot of the table. . . .

Monday February 10th

I HAVE BEEN HAPPY ALL DAY!!!

Still don't want to die, but I have a feeling it's all in hand.

Insisted we all went to the cinema tonight. When

we got there we found it was a choice between 'Confessions of a Brain-damaged Tomato', and 'Lucky the Lonely Raccoon'.

Didn't want to just go home again, so we watched the raccoon film. Anne and I quite enjoyed it, but Gerald said he used the time to work out that Sheila Walsh is an anagram of 'Lah, she wails!'

Thank goodness none of these people will ever see my diary!

Tuesday February 11th

On the way home today, met Mr Lamberton-Pincney, who runs a little group called 'Spot it and Stop it' in the church. They look for things to ban. Mr Lamberton-Pincney, who insists on his full name at all times, said that the group's annual outing was due this week, but as yet the nature of the event was undecided.

Told him about the cinema. I said, 'There's ''Confessions of a Brain-damaged Tomato'' on Studio One.' Mr Lamberton-Pincney winced in horror. 'Or there's a sort of nature film on at Studio Two.'

'Hmmm. . . ,' he said, 'that *might* be appropriate. You are sure it is not—unsuitable?'

'Oh, yes,' I said, 'Anne and Gerald and I saw it last night. It's just a film about wild creatures doing —well, wild things. Real family entertainment.'

Mr Lamberton-Pincney said that he would probably take his group to the film on Friday evening. 'You are *sure*,' he said as we parted, 'that it is a *suitable* film?'

'Oh, yes,' I replied airily, 'quite harmless.'

66

Wednesday February 12th

Edwin rang this morning to say that there's going to be a special healing meeting on Wednesday week, led by a visiting speaker from the north. Places would be limited, so did I want to reserve some seats? Said I'd ring back in five minutes. Lay on my back on the hall floor with the soles of my shoes against the front door, and after wriggling about a bit, discovered that my legs were exactly the same length as each other. Wish I'd realised that Anne and Gerald were watching from the kitchen. I'd like to have ten pounds for every time I've seen that mixture of compassion and anxiety on their faces when they look at me.

Gerald strolled into the hall with a sort of therapeutic casualness, and said, 'Don't worry, Dad. We won't let anyone in that you don't want to see.'

Silly boy! He must have *known* there was a rational explanation. told him about Edwin's call.

'The thing is,' I explained, 'that most of these healing meetings nowadays seem to end up with a lot of sick people finding that the root of their problems is one leg being longer than the other, so I was just checking mine before ringing Edwin back.'

'And . . . ?' said Anne, who'd joined us.

'Well . . . I think they're the same, so I'll call him back and say I'd like to go.'

'And if one *had* been shorter than the other?' asked Gerald, looking even more puzzled.

'Well, then I wouldn't have gone, of course,' I replied, trying not to sound too impatient.

'In case you got healed?' queried Anne.

'Exactly! What could be more embarrassing?'

Rang Edwin and asked him to reserve three seats,

then left for work, conscious that Anne and Gerald were still standing in the hall staring blankly at me as I went out of the door.

Not the first time I've noticed this dullness of intellect, especially in Gerald. Quite recently, for instance, he tried to persuade me that I should buy my petrol at a different garage a little further away, because they charge a few pence per gallon less than my usual one. I pointed out to him that as I always buy five pounds worth of petrol, the difference in price per gallon wouldn't affect me. Talk about stubborn! He ended up kneeling on the floor punching cushions. Just couldn't accept being wrong. Still—he's young.

Thursday February 13th

Gloria Marsh came to the study-group tonight. Doesn't often come.

A very attractive widowed lady.

Not that I'm in the slightest attracted to her of course, though I do think *she* has a bit of a thing about *me*. When she came in Gerald leaned over and whispered, 'Pull your stomach in, Dad, Gloria's here.'

Ridiculous!

When old Mrs Thynn said, in the course of discussion, that she had been a believer from childhood to adultery, everyone smiled, but Gloria *winked* at me! Tried to look shocked and disapproving in a desirable sort of way. Not easy. Really embarrassed later on when someone asked Gloria to describe what Christian forgiveness really meant. She said it meant that when someone smacks you on the bottom you have to turn the other cheek. Although she wasn't looking at me when she said this, I could feel my face reddening for some reason. Hope no-one noticed.

At coffee time Gloria made a beeline for me, and was soon confiding in me her problems about a large telephone bill which is beyond her means. Suddenly occurred to me that I could help. Popped upstairs and wrote a cheque, then handed it to Gloria just as she left. Went through to the kitchen and told Anne.

'You should've seen her face,' I said, 'surprised isn't the word.'

'I'm quite *sure* it isn't, dear,' said Anne, rather tartly, I thought.

Gloria rang a little later, reversing the charges, to thank me again for the money. Called me a honey-pot. Said to Anne jokingly, 'Why don't you ever call me a honey-pot, Anne?'

She said, 'Because you're not one, darling.'

Friday February 14th

Woke at 6.00 a.m., and remembered with a shock that today is Valentine's day. Dragged my clothes on as quietly as I could, crept out of the house, and staggered up to the corner shop.

Found a little clutch of haggard-looking husbands sorting through the remaining Valentine cards. Ended up with a card that had a picture on the front of a cow's backside, with the cow looking round and saying 'I LOVE YOU'. Then, when you opened the card, it said, 'FROM THE HEART OF MY BOTTOM'.

When Anne opened it at breakfast-time she said, 'Oh, darling, you're an incurable romantic. You must have spent hours choosing this.'

She laughed though. Gave me a beautiful card and

a long lingering kiss over the marmalade, interrupted by Gerald coming in and saying, 'Your tie's coming to a sticky end, Dad.'

Intrigued to see that Gerald received one of those huge padded cards, with an enormous velvet heart on the front, and hundreds of kisses done in biro on the inside. No name, though.

I said, 'Who's the secret admirer then, Gerald?'

'It's probably a joint offering from all the local girls,' he answered coolly, but you could tell he was pleased. Gerald's never had a real girlfriend—not that I'm worried about that.

Why should I be? I'm not. Never have been.

Rather surprised tonight to see that Elsie walked home from band practice with Gerald, to 'help carry his guitar'. Hope the girl who sent that Valentine didn't see them together. It might give her the wrong idea and put her off. Stupid of Elsie, when she's so devoted to William.

Saturday February 15th

Woke up with one of those rare, everything's-alright feelings. Strolled down to the shop for a loaf of bread after breakfast. Walking back, couldn't help reflecting that, although I might make the odd small mistake from time to time, generally speaking I get things right.

Felt quite a warm glow inside despite the cold.

Disconcerted to discover, when I got back to my front gate and glanced through the living-room window, that Mr Lamberton-Pincney was there, sitting on our most uncomfortable chair, and looking *very* grim.

Hid in the garage for a while reading the sports

news in a ten-year-old newspaper and hoping he'd go away. Driven in by the cold in the end. Last bit of warm glow evaporated as Anne met me at the door and hissed, 'You're an idiot! You're an absolute pea-brained dumbo! Why didn't you check they'd be showing the same film on Friday that they showed on Monday? I don't understand how you can be so stupid!'

Gathered something had gone pretty wrong.

Mr Lamberton-Pincney addressed me in Vincent Price tones.

'Following your guidance, Mr Plass,' he said ominously, 'myself and my little group attended the Studio Two cinema presentation yesterday. Being a little late, we purchased our tickets hurriedly, and entered without pausing to peruse the customary publicity material. After all . . .'

He fixed me with an accusing frown.

'We had the word of a brother Christian that the entertainment was not . . . unsuitable.'

Cleared my throat nervously. 'What err . . . was the err . . . actual film that you actually err . . . ?'

Mr Lamberton-Pincney braced himself. 'The film, Mr Plass, was entitled 'Hot Thighs in Wet Grass'.

Tried to explain and apologise. Mr Lamberton-Pincney accepted my apology heavily, then left, glancing suspiciously to left and right when he reached the road, as though he was frightened of being run over by something obscene.

'There's one thing, Dad' said Gerald, who'd been listening outside the door, 'you did tell Mr Thingummy-Whatsit the film was about wild creatures doing wild things . . .'

'And . . . ?'

'Well, from what I've heard about Hot Thighs in

Wet Grass, that'll be exactly what he saw!'

Anne called out from the kitchen, 'Where's my loaf?'

Thought for a moment. 'In the garage,' I called back.

Anne came through and stood staring at me.

Gerald said gently, 'You'll never get the car in the bread bin you know, Dad.'

Anne went off muttering, 'It won't be the *bread* bin he ends up in . . .'

Sunday February 16th

Wish there was an easy way of knowing when thoughts are just thoughts, and not messages from God. Had a thought just after quiet-time today. Just came into my head suddenly.

'Buy a tree-frog and call it Kaiser Bill.'

Sounds utterly absurd, but why should a thought like that just pop up from nowhere? Was going to tell Anne and Gerald but decided (especially after yesterday) I would just be inviting ridicule, like Richard and his impaled jellyfish. I've written the words down on a piece of paper, and put it in the inside pocket of my second best suit. After all, you never know!

Off to church.

Found that old Ephraim Trench, one of the local farmers was preaching.

Only preaches twice a year or so. Dear old fellow, but makes a real meal out of saying hardly anything at all.

Stood up today after the worship, took out a huge silver pocket-watch on a chain, checked it against the wall-clock, checked it again against Edwin's wristwatch, checked it once more to be sure against young Vernon Rawling's amazing digital chronometer, which Gerald says would probably cook a three course meal for you if you pressed the buttons in the right order, then laid the watch solemnly down on the table in front of him, and drew from his trouser pocket an enormous white handkerchief.

Treated us to a virtuoso display of nose-blowing such as has never before been seen or heard in our church. Seemed to go on for hours. Featured very fair impressions of most known wind instruments, varying from long high trumpeting blasts, to deep, sonorous, tuba-like effects. At last the old man tucked the sheet-size piece of material back into his pocket, and was just about to pick up his Bible, when the clock struck the hour and Ephraim, after counting the strokes carefully, picked his pocket-watch up again and made further minute adjustments before replacing it on the table. One or two people who'd had nothing to say Hallelujah about for ten minutes, were getting a bit restless, especially as, for one awful moment, it looked as if the old chap was going for the handkerchief pocket again, but it was a false alarm. With maddening slowness, he drew his spectacles out of the other trouser pocket, cleaned them meticulously with a soft cloth, and finally put them on. Picked up his well-thumbed old Authorised Version, and peered sternly round the room like an old-fashioned Sunday School teacher.

'Roight!' he said, ''ere we go! 'Smornin' we're gonna look at a psalm ain't we? We're gonna look at psalm twenny-three! An' oi'm 'appy to say, the Lorrrd 'as revealed to me a way of foindin' it quick-like in moi bible, an' oi'm gonna pass it on to all of you 'ere 'smornin'! It goes loike—as follers.'

Ephraim spoke in prophetic tones.

'Psalm twenny-three can easily be found moi brothers an' sisters, 'cause the Lorrrd in 'is wisdom 'as placed it immediate after psalm twenny-two an' just previous to psalm twenny-four! Allylooyer!'

Gerald and Anne and I said 'Hallelujah!' very loudly to support Ephraim. He's a good old chap.

Elsie round this afternoon to ask Gerald's advice about a song she's writing. Must be taking her music very seriously to give up an afternoon when she could have been with William. Gerald showed me a copy of her song later. It begins like this:

I'm in love with someone special,
He means so much to me,
He's a very lovely person,
And his name begins with 'G'.

Said to Anne tonight how great I thought it was that a girl of Elsie's age could write such a positive song about God. She looked at me rather oddly. Don't know why.

Monday February 17th

Something interesting this evening. Heard next door's front gate click open and clang shut, and when I looked out of the hall window (to see what the weather was doing) I saw that monk, Father John, waiting at Frank Braddock's front door. Rushed through to the kitchen and found some empty milk bottles to put out on the step. Got out there just in time to see Braddock throw open his door, and shout, 'Bungles! Well, stap me vitals! Come on in, mate.'

The monk, chuckling, and saying something that

sounded like, 'Avast there, Smelly', disappeared into the house and shut the door behind him.

Interesting!!

Felt a twinge of my old back trouble this evening. Hope it doesn't get any worse. I'd hate to miss that healing meeting on Wednesday week. I want to actually *see* someone being healed.

Tuesday February 18th

Spent a pleasant hour with the Doves after work today. Kitty rather poorly, but still twinkling and smiling. Told them about my problems over dying and going to heaven and messing up Mr Thingummybob-Pincney's outing and—well, everything really. Bill said I was a very unusual person, and Kitty said God must be using all these mistakes and problems to train me up for a special job that only I could do. Never thought of it like that. Felt quite bright when I left.

Bill walked down to the front gate with me, and told me quietly that Kitty's going into hospital soon for tests, but she doesn't want a fuss made.

Told Anne and Gerald about Kitty when I got home. I said a little prayer, and we all said 'Amen!', louder than usual.

Leonard round to play Scrabble with Gerald and I tonight. I got told off for taking too long as usual and Leonard kept putting down words like 'vquex', which, according to Thynn, is defined in the full length Oxford Dictionary as 'a cross between a ferret and a giraffe'. Gerald objected on the grounds that the mating act would be geometrically impossible between two such animals, and the rest of the conversation became rather more ribaldly vulgar than

I care to record in what is after all a Christian diary.

Back still a little painful. Laughed immoderately on the stairs when Gerald said that Gavin Reid is an anagram of 'vain dirge', and gave it a bit of a twist.

Wednesday February 19th

Can't help worrying that Gerald's getting obsessional about these anagrams. Came downstairs at one o'clock this morning after hearing a noise, and found Gerald still up in the sitting room clutching a pencil and surrounded by pieces of paper with letters scribbled all over them. Looked at me with wild triumphant eyes, and said 'Vile creed!'

Backed off a bit nervously.

'Eric Delve!' he said, waving one of the sheets of paper. 'Eric Delve is an anagram of Vile creed!'

Went back to bed. Honestly! Stupid boy!

Felt led during quiet-time this morning, to give poor, quaint old Mr Brain, our ex-actor neighbour, a little financial gift. Remembered that verse in the bible about giving secretly. Didn't even tell Anne what I was doing. Popped it through his letterbox in a plain envelope when I got home from work. Hung about for a bit, hoping he'd spot me through the window.

Edwin popped in tonight. Says he's invited a special guest speaker, Dwight Hackenbacker, who's a Californian, to talk about the 'Gifts', on Sunday.

Thursday February 20th

Couldn't help feeling a sort of glow inside all day at work, thinking of Mr Brain's pleasure. What a joy and a privilege it is to give!!

Had a discussion at study-group tonight about unity in the church, and whether it was a good thing or not. Richard Cook said he didn't mind as long as we didn't have to change the way we worship, or mix with people from other churches who were not 'truly in The Way'.

Old Mrs Thynn said that she didn't mind getting together with other Christians, but she didn't want to have to go into the sort of churches where you walked through the door and 'all you could smell was incest'.

We all laughed, but Edwin said we should take this important subject seriously, and reflect on the fact that we are all parts of the Body of the church, and therefore need each other.

Good discussion after that, ending with each of us saying what part of the body we thought we were. Anne started, by saying that she thought she was probably a bit of dried skin on the elbow, but Edwin, bless him, said that he thought she was much nearer the *heart* than that.

Haven't seen Anne blush like that for ages!

Rather fortunately, I thought, Gerald got up to answer the telephone in the hall at this point. As he squeezed past Richard, he said, 'Excuse me Richard, but you are truly in the way.'

We all agreed that Edwin is an ear, because he's good at listening, and George Farmer said he knew he was a mouth. Thynn said he was a left shoulder blade for some obscure reason, and Norma Twill said she thought she might be a dimple. Couldn't think what *I* was, and dismissed Thynn's assessment of me as a small, unimportant vein in the right foot. All good fun really!

Gerald reappeared just as we were winding up, and said he'd thought of a good name for the church if all the denominations formed a united group.

'It's simple,' he said, 'we'll call ourselves the Maptocostal Angloholics!'

Asked Gerald later who he'd been on the phone to all that time.

'Oh,' he said, 'that was Elsie ringing up to say she'd finished her song, and just . . . chatting.'

Quite pleased really. Must be good for a girl like Elsie to have a close platonic friendship with a member of the opposite sex. Said this to Anne at bedtime. She laughed and said something quite inexplicable.

'Darling, if you ever decide to have a secret affair, you'd better let me organise it.'

Friday February 21st

Came home from work tonight to find a note on the mat addressed to me.

Dear Mr Plass,

In the remote past you took possession of my excellent mechanical hedge trimmer. You described the transaction as a 'loan'. Possibly the terms 'loan' and 'theft' are synonymous in your vocabulary. If not, perhaps you would return my property. Otherwise I must invite you to explain your verbal idiosyncrasies to my solicitors, from whom you will shortly hear.

From your frail elderly victim,

Percival X Brain.

Showed it to Anne. She said, 'What a scream! He's a real character, isn't he?'

I said, 'Yes, Anne. He's a real character.'

Took the blasted trimmer round to the silly old fool. When he came to the door I said, 'Anything good happened this week, Mr Brain?'

Brain said, 'The Lord has provided, young man, through some soul whose nature it is to give rather than take. A lesson there for *you*, Plass! A lesson!'

Wagged his finger at me. I nearly trimmed it. Went home and sulked for an hour. In the end Anne tickled me from behind and said, 'Aaah . . . Diddums got the sulkie-wulkies 'cos nasty Mr Brainy-Wainy finks diddums is a big nasty man. . . .'

Couldn't help smiling. Sulk ruined.

Gerald in late tonight from B.N.F.T.D. practice, looking very thoughtful. Asked him what was up. He said, 'Nothing for you to worry your pretty little head about, Dad. Just band stuff—you know.'

Saturday February 22nd

Secret giving's hard!!!

At the moment I feel like strangling Brain, and telling him about the money just before he dies. Fine Christian I am! Asked God to make me a better person.

No noticeable improvement by this evening.

So there can't be a God after all, can there?

1.30 a.m. Didn't mean that last bit. Just being flippant. Course there is.

Sunday February 23rd

To church.

Dwight Hackenbacker, the Californian, spoke powerfully about Word of Knowledge. He said it was a gift for today's church, and that we could all practise it 'RIGHT NOW!' if we really wanted to.

There was a short silence, then young Vernon Rawlings stood up, pointed dramatically at Ephraim Trench's youngest girl, Bessie, and said, 'You've got a pain in your lower abdomen!'

Bessie went pink and said she hadn't.

Vernon said she had.

Bessie said she hadn't.

Vernon said she had.

Then Bessie said she hadn't, and she should know because it was *her* lower abdomen.

Vernon said that he *knew* she had a pain in her lower abdomen, and perhaps she didn't have the faith to feel it. Edwin stepped in then, thank goodness. I think if I'd heard the words 'lower abdomen' once more I'd have gone mad.

At coffee time some people seemed a bit confused. Deaf old Mrs Thynn asked Dwight if Word of Knowledge was made by the same people as Cluedo and Monopoly, becuase she'd like to give it to her grandson for his birthday.

Left early, feeling flat. Brain on my mind.

Monday February 24th

Edwin popped in just after tea. 'Just to tell you,' he said, 'how pleased the Lord is about your generosity to Mr Brain.'

I just stared. 'How on earth did . . . ?'

Edwin smiled. 'You were at church on Sunday, weren't you? See you later!'

Went round to Mr Brain's house later. Said I'd come to see if there was anything I could do for him. He said the most useful thing I could do was drink a pint of his home-made bitter, and listen to some stories about his experiences as a 'thespian'.

Awful beer, but I drank every drop. Excellent stories—enjoyed every word. As I left he said, 'I would be obliged, young man, if in the future, you would address me as "Percy", a more informal, and significantly less cranial term than "Brain". By the way, I feel it incumbent upon me to offer you something in the way of an apology for the style and content of my recent communication to you. The fact is . . .'

The old man suddenly looked very vulnerable.

'The fact is that I am, as it were, devoid of familial comforts, and I had entertained hopes that the loan of my trimming machine might have signalled the commencement of a . . . might have marked the genesis of . . . of a relationship. I fear that disappointment was the main motivator for my somewhat aggressive missal. Perhaps we might now consider ourselves to have embarked on a . . . on a . . .'

'Friendship?', I suggested.

'Precisely!' said Percy, beaming happily. 'A friendship. Precisely! Ale and conversation! We shall be friends and brothers!'

Isn't God nice sometimes!

(I mean *all* the time, of course. Sorry God.)

Tuesday February 25th

Got up early this morning to check the length of my legs again, ready for the healing meeting tomorrow night. As far as I can reasonably tell, they are absolutely identical, so that's that.

Confessed everything I could possibly think of in my quiet-time, so that no-one in the meeting can minister to some secret sin in my life, and did a few exercises to check my back's alright. No pain at all, so it's all systems go for tomorrow. I'd just like to see one person really healed. That would be really amazing! Not an internal organ or something that you can't see. I want to see someone get out of a wheelchair, or throw away their crutches—that sort of thing.

Not that I don't believe God can do it, of course. I know he can. He *does* do it! I've read about it. I just . . . want to see it.

Gerald has suggested we have a party soon. Anne thinks it's a good idea too, so we've decided to have it on Friday week, as long as the rest of Gerald's band don't mind missing a practice.

Gerald said, 'Is it going to be a Christian party or a real party?'

Didn't know what he meant.

'What do you mean by a Christian party?'

'*You* know,' he said, 'all flans and fruit juice. Let's have some french bread, and different cheeses and a few bottles of plonk, then we can ask all sorts of people.'

I know what Gerald means, but there are some of my non-Christian friends who I'd be a bit nervous about putting in the same room as a lot of wine and some of my *Christian* friends. I'll have to give it some thought.

Wednesday February 26th

Went through yesterday morning's routine again today. All well. Roll on tonight!

Set off to walk down to Unity Hall with Gerald and Anne at about 7.15. Felt quite excited really. Our seats were around the middle, not too far forward. The evening started with choruses, led by one of those people who Gerald says have 'A' levels in Ecstasy. All very enjoyable until someone went up to the front and whispered something into the ecstatic fellow's ear. When she'd finished, he spoke to us in one of those close-to-the-microphone voices.

'That sister has shared with me her feeling that the Lord is saying there are folk here who are not released in physical expression of their joy. He would have them know the joy of true freedom in worship.'

Adopted my expression of prayerful calm concern.

Took years to develop—absolutely essential in this sort of situation. With a slight swaying motion that could possibly be construed as dancing, and a subdued but dignified handclap, I can get through most of these awful periods without too much trouble.

Gerald is much cruder. Just ignores it all. He leaned over and whispered in my ear.

'We'll find that "sister" afterwards, and duff her up, shall we?'

Disappointed to note, as the speaker rose to his feet at last, that there were no wheelchairs or crutches in evidence. Still, you can't have everything.

Jolly good, simple talk by the speaker. Very down to earth—northern accent. At the end of his main talk, he said, 'Right, now it's not much use coming down here and talking about how God can heal, if at the end of it all, nobody is. So let's have a look at you!'

Sat back happily, confident in the knowledge that my legs were the same length and my back didn't hurt.

He said, 'Right, first of all there's a young lady here who has injured her arm in the kitchen this morning. The Lord's going to sort it out, so step up quick, we've got a lot to get through.'

A girl stood up looking dazed and incredulous, and went up to the front. She had a bandage on her arm. After he'd prayed over the arm, the speaker said, 'Well, come on, take the bandage off! Hold your arm up and let 'em all see what God's done for you!'

She held her bare arm up and said, 'It's . . . it's better!'

'Course it's better,' he said, 'sit down yer daft thing!'

Suddenly felt scared. Hadn't banked on there really being a God who really told people real things about real people. Wanted to hide. But where?

'. . . and now I think there's a couple of folk with back problems. One of them's a bruise at the base of the spine . . .'

Relief! Mine had been much higher up near the shoulder-blades. Phew!

'. . . and the other is much higher up near the shoulder-blades . . .'

Oh, no! But I wasn't actually in pain . . .

'. . . and it's not painful just now, but every now and then it gives you some real stick.'

The bruised base of the spine surfaced and was dealt with pretty quickly, then told to go for a run round the car park to make sure it was really healed.

A silence fell. Nearly jumped out of my skin when Gerald leaned across and tapped me on the knee.

'Go on, Dad,' he said quietly, 'It's you—you know it is!'

No escape! Trailed reluctantly up to the front, and whispered urgently to the speaker.

'My legs are exactly the same length you know!'

'Well that's useful—for things like walking,' he whispered back, with a broad grin.

'And my back's not hurting at all at the moment,' I added.

'Great!' he said, 'and it's not going to hurt you in the future either.'

Put his hands on my back and prayed. Felt a sort of heat go through me, but nothing else. As I turned to go back to my seat, he whispered, 'God likes you, lad, he really does!'

No really dramatic healings after that.

When we got home I rang Bill Dove and told him what had happened.

'The thing is, Bill,' I said, 'I was scared when it looked as if God was really there and really did exist.

So does that mean I never really believed in him before?'

Heard Bill chuckle at the other end of the phone.

'Doesn't mean any such thing,' he said. 'It just means that up to now you've had faith bunged away in your heart, but tonight you had it shoved into your head. Always a bit of a shock. You'll handle it—don't worry.'

I said, 'How's Kitty, Bill?'

'Booked for home, I'd say,' said Bill quietly. 'I reckon she's booked for home.'

Thursday February 27th

I wish dirty jokes weren't so funny sometimes. Heard one this morning from Everett Glander who works at the next desk to me. Really side-splitting!

All about General Custer, a mackerel, and lots of Indians. My usual polite-smile-followed-by-a-tut-of-distaste almost didn't work. Glander does it on purpose because he knows I'm a Christian. He's enjoyed baiting me ever since the time when I had a bit too much at the office party two years ago, and he came up and said, 'How about us talking about *my* beliefs for once?'

After a year of crinkling my eyes into a Christian smile every time he asked his incessant questions about 'Who made God?', and 'What about suffering?', I'd run out of patience, and with four unwise pints of best bitter inside me, I looked at Glander, hated him, and said, 'Stuff your beliefs!'

Apologised later, but he's cashed in ever since.

All the same—pity there's no-one I *can* tell the General Custer joke to. It's *so* funny! Toyed with the idea of telling it to the study-group as an example of the sort of joke we shouldn't tell as Christians. Decided it wouldn't go down too well, really.

(Memo—Everett Glander is precisely the sort of person I *don't* want at this party of ours. The thought of him telling his awful jokes, and letting all my Christian friends know that I once got drunk and told him to stuff his beliefs, makes me go all hot and cold.)

Good tape at study-group tonight, by a man who does Christian meditation. Apparently he gets up very early every Saturday morning, and meditates on something like 'eternity', or 'love', or 'creation' for anything up to two hours. He says the rest of the weekend is filled with a special kind of peace for him and his family as a result. Think I'll try it this Saturday.

Do wish Leonard would make his mother turn her hearing aid up when she comes to meetings. When the tape finished, and Edwin asked for comments, she said, 'Well, I feel sorry for 'im. I should think 'e can 'ardly move with all that lot sloshin' around inside 'im. Wouldn't make me feel peaceful!'

After a long blank silence, it turned out that she thought the man on the tape had said he took *medication* for two hours every morning. Anne had to explain in the corner for ages. I dunno!

No sign of Gloria Marsh again this evening. Not that it matters to me personally, of course. Mentioned to Anne that Gloria hasn't been for two weeks.

She said, 'Perhaps she finds you so irresistible, darling, that she decided to do the sensible thing and keep away.'

How ludicrous! That's almost certainly *not* the reason!

Friday February 28th

Nearly told Gerald the Custer/mackerel/Indian joke at breakfast this morning. Felt guilty at the last moment and didn't.

Spent part of my lunch hour today thinking about the party next Friday. Pity they don't sell anti-invitation cards.

> Dear Everett Glander,
>   We are holding a party on
>   Friday next, and would be
>   very pleased if you would
>   not attend, as your presence
>   would be embarrassing and
>   unwelcome.
>   Yours, very sincerely, etc.

Couldn't help chuckling at the thought. Glander heard me and said, 'Still thinking about the old Custer joke? Good'n', eh? Told it to the wife yet?'

'I wouldn't consider passing a joke of that type on to anyone,' I said, with the sorrowful smile I use for Everett. 'I don't really find jokes of that kind very funny I'm afraid, Everett.'

'What *were* you laughing at then?' said Everett in the persistent way he has sometimes. 'Some nice clean Christian joke?'

Suddenly went cold and guilty inside. I'd been laughing about the idea of sending a cruel, nasty letter to the man I worked next to every day. The Custer joke didn't seem all that bad in comparison. Cleared my throat.

'Actually, Everett, I was thinking about a party we're having next Friday. Anne and I would . . .

would be pleased if you could come and . . . well come.'

Never seen him so taken aback.

'You're asking me to a party at *your* house next Friday?'

'Yes—and your wife, of course. About eight o'clock if that's okay.'

'Well, yes,' said Everett, eyes still screwed up in puzzlement. 'Yes, I'm sure we'd love to come. Bring a stock of funnies and a couple of bottles of holy water, eh?'

Felt quite good about this at the time, but it wore off. Haven't dared tell Anne Everett's coming.

'Funnies and Holy water.'

WHAT HAVE I DONE??!!

12.30 a.m.

Had intended to go to bed early so as to be wide awake at 5.00 a.m. for meditation, but got seduced by the snooker on television. Decided that if I was a famous snooker player I'd like to be known as 'Pink-ball Plass'.

To bed! I've set the alarm for 5.30, and I shall meditate until half past seven.

Saturday March 1st

Alarm clock exploded dead on 5.30 a.m.

Wondered for a moment what lunatic had set it for such a ridiculous hour, then remembered it was me. Anne half woke and said sleepily, 'Darling, *what* are you doing?'

I whispered, 'Go back to sleep, Anne. I'm just going to go and think about eternity for a couple of hours.'

As I tiptoed out of the room I distinctly heard Anne say, 'To think I had a proposal of marriage from someone normal once . . .'

Crawled downstairs and knelt, bleary eyed, in the sitting room. Put my watch on the floor in front of me so as not to carry on past seven thirty.

Started contemplating eternity at exactly 5.34 a.m. Kept my eyes shut and tried to concentrate on things going on for ever and ever. Not easy. Found my thoughts drifting off to holidays, and why you don't see those wicker waste-paper baskets any more, and what a cross between a ferret and a giraffe could possibly look like. Was just imagining a creature with a ferret's body, and a neck so long that it could put its head right down a rabbit hole without moving its legs, when I remembered what I was *supposed* to be thinking about. Clenched my mind and really tried hard. After about an hour, opened my eyes to check the time. It was 5.44 a.m.

Thought about eternity for another couple of minutes, but my head began to ache. Tried going back to bed but I couldn't sleep. Got up again. Anne came down at a quarter to eight.

She said, 'Of course, you've been meditating, haven't you, darling? How much of your two hours did you do?'

'Twelve minutes,' I said.

Told her I'd been too tired and my head hurt.

'But you came to bed so late,' she said, 'no wonder you were too tired.'

Afraid I've been bad tempered and sulky all day since then. Obviously twelve minutes isn't long enough to produce that 'special kind of peace' for oneself and one's family. Spent quite a long time out the back this afternoon, talking to Brenda, our rabbit.

She might think I'm irritable and annoying, but she can't say so.

Sunday March 2nd

Forgot to get fruit-gums at the corner shop on the way to church today. Felt occupationally naked during Edwin's talk on the authority of the Bible. Slightly enlivened at the end when Edwin said that some books were apocryphal, and old Mrs Thynn said in a very loud voice, 'A pocket full of what?'

Spent the afternoon and evening with Anne writing out our invitations to the party. We seem to have invited an awful lot of people, Christians *and* non-Christians.

Hope it'll be alright! Still haven't told Anne about Glander. Still, there's one comfort—Uncle Ralph's not invited, and he's too far away to hear about it in any other way. That would be *too* much!

Asked Anne this evening whether she believed every word of the Bible was true. She said she'd always had to wrestle with profound doubts about one particular semi-colon half way through Zephaniah. Said I thought this was nit-picking, but she just burst into laughter and asked how we were going to keep Thynn away from the booze on Friday. Good point. How?

Asked Gerald the same question about the Bible later on.

'Well,' he said, 'I tend to go along with the views of St. Boglash of Flinge, who wrote a fascinating 53 volume work on the use of the apostrophe in Bible literature. He died in 1371 when a set of his own volumes fell on him as he knelt at prayer and . . .'

'Okay, okay!' I interrupted. 'No need to go on.

I'm not that stupid. I know perfectly well there's no such place as Flinge.'

Had him there! He really looked taken aback. I only *pretend* to be naive from time to time.

Prayed for Kitty again tonight. Surely God doesn't want someone like her to die . . .

Monday March 3rd

At breakfast Anne said, 'I've got a little confession to make, darling.'

Don't have many opportunities to be magnanimously forgiving towards Anne. Felt rather pleased in a way. Leaned over the table and took her hand.

'Whatever it is, I forgive you in advance,' I said. Smiled encouragingly.

Anne said, 'I've invited Uncle Ralph to the party.'

Quite flabbergasted! 'Anne, how could you?' I shouted. 'Are you mad?! Ralph doesn't just *lower* the tone of a party, he buries it! Why on earth did you do such a stupid thing? You must be off your head! you stupid, stupid . . .'

SUDDENLY REMEMBERED I'D INVITED EVERETT GLANDER!!

Could see Anne's lower lip trembling.

'I'm awfully sorry, darling,' she said with a little sob. 'It's j-just that he's all alone and no-one really l-likes him and it suddenly seemed so m-mean not to . . . I *know* it was silly, but . . . you did say you'd forgive me in advance . . .'

Knew I'd be lucky to leave the room alive.

'Oh, I just over-reacted,' I said airily. 'After all, we all do silly thing from time to time.' Stood up and edged towards the door. 'Take me, for instance. You may have invited Uncle Ralph, but I've . . . I've invited . . . I have actually invited . . .'

'Oh, no . . .' said Anne, 'Not him—surely not him! Tell me you haven't invited that awful Glander man to our party!'

Both started to laugh suddenly—thank goodness!

'Uncle Ralph and Everett Glander,' I said. 'God help us!'

'I'm banking on that,' said Anne.

Noticed Anne and Gerald whispering together at teatime. Asked what was going on. Anne said, 'How's your back, darling?'

'Fine,' I said, 'Why?'

They just smiled at each other.

Another odd incident later on. Elsie came round at about half-past seven to tell Gerald that William had managed to book Unity Hall for a practice tomorrow night instead of Friday, then stayed chatting for a while. I said, 'Has Gerald told you about the big Valentine's card he got this year, Elsie? Some cow-eyed girl's really got it bad for this young man! Go and get it Gerald—show it to Elsie, it's hilarious! The poor girl must be a bit simple. She spent hours doing hundreds of tiny kisses in biro. Gerald and I were in fits, weren't we Gerald? I bet you wouldn't go to all that trouble for your William. Did *you* send *him* a card this year?'

Suddenly realised, as I finished speaking, that these perfectly harmless comments were producing rather odd responses.

Elsie was bright red, opening and shutting her mouth like a goldfish, and Gerald had screwed his eyes shut like you do just before a crash. Felt, in some inexplicable way, that I'd lost my Claire Raynor image. Anne called me into the kitchen just then, so I didn't get a chance to ask what was wrong. These young people!

(*Another* odd thing. When I got to the kitchen Anne had forgotten why she called me, but was annoyed with *me* instead of herself! I can't help thinking now and then, that I'm surrounded by some very funny people!)

Tuesday March 4th

Hadn't planned to go down to the band practice tonight, but Anne said the way things were with Gerald and Elsie, perhaps we ought to be there. Couldn't think what she was on about, but she's usually right, so off we went.

Terrible atmosphere when we got there. William Farmer sitting in a corner on one of those minuscule play-group chairs, looking very black indeed, Vernon Rawlings draped over a radiator picking his ear with a plectrum, and Gerald leaning against the wall, gazing at the ceiling and whistling tunelessly to himself. No sign of Elsie. It all looked like very *good* news for the devil, whatever *it* was.

Was just going to say something, when Elsie came out of the Ladies, red-eyes and sniffing. Homes in on me like an exocet missile.

'Mr Plass!' she said dramatically. 'You tried to push William and I together a month ago when you must have realised we were never really suited . . .'

'But you asked me to . . .'

' . . . and I want to tell you—I feel *led* to tell you that however much you may try to keep us apart, Gerald and I are *meant* for each other!'

Glanced at Anne in bewilderment, but she looked as if she already knew what was going on!

She said, 'Elsie, my love, if you and Gerald want to go out together, that's fine with us, absolutely fine—honestly it is.'

'Fine . . .', I echoed feebly.

Elsie revved furiously in neutral for a moment, then, obviously feeling we were sufficiently cowed, turned to Gerald and said, 'It's going to be alright, Gerald darling!'

'Oh, err . . . good, good,' said Gerald. 'That's err . . . good, Elsie.'

The dark figure in the corner grunted sardonically.

Anne moved over to speak quietly to William.

Felt a bit troubled really. Didn't like the idea of our Gerald trailing submissively behind a sort of female Rambo. Needn't have worried. Gerald put his hands on Elsie's shoulders, looked deep into her eyes, and said, 'Elsie, there's something I want to tell you— something I want you always to remember. Promise you'll never forget what I'm about to tell you.'

Elsie's eyes shone.

'Of course, Gerald! I promise I'll never forget!'

'Well then . . .' He paused. Vernon suspended his ear picking.

'Yes Gerald?' Elsie's eyes couldn't have opened wider.

'I want you to know,' continued Gerald in a deep throbbing voice, 'that Mother-in-law is an anagram of Woman Hitler. Never forget that!'

By the time we left, the band—including William, who seemed almost miraculously restored to good spirits—had launched itself frenziedly into one of its orchestrated epileptic fits, and everything seemed more or less normal again.

Asked Anne on the way home, what she said to William to perk him up so quickly.

'Oh,' she said, 'I just told him that if he put all the raw passion he feels about Elsie into his music, he'll be the nearest thing to a Christian Meatloaf that anyone's ever heard . . .'

'What's a Christian Meatloaf, for heavens sake?'

'. . . and I told him that if I was a teenager, I'd be at the front of the queue now, and glad to see the back of Elsie, especially as she never did *really* understand him. That's what I told him.'

'What's a Christian Meatloaf?'

'Ask Gerald later, darling. He knows more about it than I do.'

Asked Gerald later, 'What's a Christian Meatloaf?'

He said, 'Mum means he could become something big in heavy metal. I don't personally think he's quite in the "Bat out of hell" class, though, do you?'

Something big in heavy metal?

Not in the 'Bat out of hell' class?

Are we all going mad???

Never mind, Gerald's got a girlfriend, so he's certainly not gay.

(Not that I ever thought he *was*.)

Wednesday March 5th

(Not that I'm prejudiced against gay people.)

Rang Leonard up and arranged to meet him for lunch (not in a pub!). Before getting round to the subject of the party, I asked him what he'd ended up thinking after Edwin's talk on Sunday. He looked pleased. Doesn't usually get asked for an opinion. Overdid it of course. Leaned back in his chair, put his fingertips together and tried to look wise.

'Well, I did sit right up at the front on Sunday.'

'Yes.'

'So I was very close to Edwin as he talked.'

'Yes . . .'

'And I did end up doing something I'd never quite managed before.'

'Yes—and that was . . . ?'

'I counted Edwin's teeth. He's got thirty-six.'

Thynn amazes me. Seems an awful shame to waste all that space in his head. Gave up and asked him what he was going to do about drinking at the party. Leonard loves parties.

'Well,' he said, 'I've just been trying a new lager-free alcohol that mother found. I'll bring some of that. We teetotallers don't want to embarrass you drinkers.'

Wasn't till I got home this evening that I realised what Leonard had said. Lager-free alcohol? He *did* mean the other way round. Didn't he? Please!!!

(Not that I think it's right.)

Thursday March 6th

(Being gay I mean.)

8.30 a.m.

Won't have much time for diary entries today. We've only got till the study-group starts, to do all the shopping for the party. Don't want to leave it till tomorrow. Norma Twill just phoned to say she's got a job interview at the marshmallow factory this afternoon and would I pray for her. Said I would, but it'll have to wait 'till I get to work now.

10.00 p.m.

I blush to record what happened at the study-group tonight. Most charitable thing I can think is that Uncle Ralph *didn't* know there was a group of people praying in the sitting room when he arrived this evening. The group had just got onto Doreen Cook's knee (praying about it I mean, not sitting on it), when a hand appeared round the door that opens from the hall, holding a pair of pink-sugar lady's legs, and a voice said in a sort of music-hall French accent, 'Voulez-vouz jig-a-jig?'

Anne leaped to her feet, pushed the hand back into the hall and followed it, closing the door behind her. There was a brief, hissed, verbal scuffle, then silence. Pretty sure everyone had seen the legs. *Absolutely* sure everyone had heard the voice.

Long embarrassed silence. Could have fried an egg on my face.

Bit difficult to concentrate on poor old Doreen's knee after that. Anne came back after a while and apologised for Uncle Ralph. Said she'd sent him to bed without any supper. Everyone except the Flushpools laughed and said it was alright, but you could see that they were all a bit shocked.

What's he going to do at the party, for goodness sake?

As they left, Norma Twill drew me aside and whispered excitedly, 'I got the job, Adrian.'

'Job?' I said, 'What job?'

Norma's face dropped.

'You know, the job! You've been praying about it for me today. I've got it! They're putting me on the pink and whites. I just wanted to thank you for praying this morning.'

'Oh, you mean *that* job!' I gabbled. 'Oh yes, of *course* I know what you mean, and congratulations! Well done!'

'Well, thank you anyway,' smiled Norma. 'I'm sure your prayers helped.'

Would have to be a very different sort of man to have admitted to Norma that I'd forgotten to pray.

'Oh, no,' I protested modestly, 'it was nothing—really nothing.'

Very troubled later. Explained to Anne.

'Perhaps you shouldn't be so quick to promise,' she said, 'but don't worry too much. *You* may not have prayed—but *I* did. You owe me half an hour of prayer!'

Good old Anne.

Rotten old Ralph.

Muddled old me.

Wish we'd never thought of having a party.

Wonder how Kitty is? Don't want to ask, really.

Friday March 7th

9.00 a.m.

Had a totally unrecordable dream last night,

provoked, I'm quite sure by Norma Twill's news that she is going to be working with those pink and white marshmallows. So vivid, I decided to tell Anne. Changed my mind and didn't.

1.00 p.m.

Sat down with Ralph this morning to lay down the law as far as the party's concerned.

'Right!' I said, 'There are a few little things I want to talk to you about, Ralph. Things like getting drunk, and making suggestive comments to ladies, and dirty stories, and vulgar practical jokes, and games involving drink, or sex, or both!'

'Fine!' said Uncle Ralph, rubbing his hands, 'You mean you want us to plan the party.'

'No,' I said, 'that's *not* what I mean, Uncle Ralph. What I *mean* is that I don't want any of those things to happen. A lot of the guests will be young Christians.'

'What am *I* then?' demanded Uncle Ralph, 'An old pagan?'

Yes, I thought, that's just what you are. 'Look, all I'm saying is that the people at the party are Christians, and they don't much like all those things I mentioned just now, so could you just chat pleasantly, have a couple of drinks, and be just—well —pleasant?'

'Just chat?'

'Yes.'

'A couple of drinks?'

'Yes.'

'No dirty stories?'

'No.'

'No practical jokes?'

'None!'

'Be pleasant?'

'Yes please.'

Uncle Ralph sighed, his little fat face a picture of gloom.

'Doesn't sound much of a party to me,' he said, 'still, I'll try.'

1.00 a.m.

Too tired to write about the party tonight. Do it tomorrow. Gerald has a strange brain. Leaned on the doorframe just now, yawned, and said, 'Did you know that Robert Runcie is an anagram of 'C.E., but in error?'

At 1.00 a.m.!!!

Saturday March 8th

11.00 a.m.

All cleared up! Mostly Anne and Gerald actually. Said they didn't wake me early because they preferred doing *all* the cleaning themselves, to being helped a *bit*, by me in a bad temper. I'm *not* like that! Got quite angry with them when they said I'm always irritable early in the morning.

Anyway . . .

Party! What a strange evening. Far as I can recall, events were as follows. Worth putting down in detail, I reckon.

7.45

No-one had arrived. Worried that nobody would come. Popped next door to borrow a few extra glasses from Percy Brain. Asked him if he was coming. Said he'd come when it had 'warmed up'. No-one ever wants to *do* the warming up!

8.00

Came back to the house to hear laughter and glass-clinking coming from the sitting-room. Uncle Ralph suddenly emerged, the old beam back on his face, and a large glass of scotch in his hand.

'Here, I say, old man, I don't half like these Christian friends of yours. The first one's just come and he's brought a bottle of whisky—this is some of it he poured for me—and he's just told me a great story about General Custer and a mackerel and some Indians. You see this bloke decided . . .'

'I've heard it!'

Just my luck! Everett Glander and Uncle Ralph getting together right at the beginning of the party. Felt like disaster, especially as the very next guest was Leonard Thynn, clutching four cans of (thankfully) alcohol-free lager, but with an excited gleam in his eye.

Next hour was like a nightmare. Anne and I spent our time welcoming guests then rushing back to the living room to prevent Leonard from drinking and Uncle Ralph and Everett from turning the whole thing into a sort of Bernard Manning show. Slipped upstairs eventually and hid in my bedroom for a few minutes to escape the noise and commotion. Suddenly realised the row had died down. Anne opened the door and said, 'Come and look!'

Went back down and listened outside the sitting room. Only one voice to be heard. Opened the door as quietly as possible and tip-toed into the corner. Frank Braddock was sitting in an armchair at the far end of the crowded room, a pint glass in one hand and his pipe in the other, talking easily to the rest of the guests, who seemed to be listening with close attention to what he was saying.

'He was a nuisance *then*,' said Braddock, 'and he's a nuisance now. He won't let you work out cosy little systems and call 'em "churches", and he won't let you get away with having four meetings a week to discuss what you're going to do in next week's meetings. If *that's* what you want, you'll find Jesus a real pain in the neck. He says awkward, difficult things, like ''Love your enemies'', and ''Invite the people who really need it to dinner'', and ''Love God before anything else''. He's terrible like that. They couldn't pin him down then, and you can't pin him down now, but I'll tell you something . . .'

Braddock leaned forward in his chair and stabbed the air with his pipe stem. His eyes were filled with excitement. Amazed to see Everett Glander and Uncle Ralph listening like small children.

'. . . if you want to pay the cost, there's no-one else worth following, and nothing else worth doing!'

Braddock took a long satisfying pull at his pint, and leaned back in his chair.

Mrs Flushpool, sitting on a hard chair at the side of the room was clearly impressed despite herself, but not entirely won over.

'Mr Braddock,' she said, 'would your message not be more convincing if you were to abstain from strong drink and noxious substances, such as tobacco? Stenneth and I neither drink nor smoke. Scripture issues grave warnings on these matters!'

(Stenneth?!)

Braddock blew a long stream of smoke towards the ceiling.

'Ah, scripture!' he said. 'Scripture certainly does warn that those whose strong faith allows them freedom in these things, must be careful not to harm those of a weaker faith who have abstained altogether.'

He held up his glass and his pipe.

'My dear Mrs Flushpool, if my drinking or my

smoking is tempting you unbearably, I shall never drink or smoke in front of you again. Say the word!'

'Stenneth and I are *not* tempted to drink or smoke, or indulge in any other vice,' said Mrs F. firmly.

'Amen to that!' responded Mr Flushpool, with just a hint of sadness in his voice.

Braddock went on speaking to the assembled guests until about 11.30. No-one got drunk, Uncle Ralph seemed quite happy, Everett Glander looked very thoughtful as he left, and the rest of the guests said how much they'd enjoyed the evening. Edwin asked Frank Braddock if he would come and speak in our church one day. Frank said he would if Edwin would come and play snooker at his club one evening. Edwin laughed and agreed.

As Frank left, I said, 'Which church do *you* go to Frank?'

'Just an ordinary local one,' he said, 'but, . . .' He smiled, '. . . I like to use the word 'church' as a verb, as well as a noun. See you! Thanks for the party. Night!'

Didn't really understand.

(No-one's called Stenneth, are they? Surely?)

Bill and Kitty Dove both got invitations to the party, though we knew they wouldn't come, of course. Rang Bill tonight, hoping he'd say Kitty was better. No change. No better, no worse. Just have to wait.

Sunday March 9th

Wouldn't ever say this to anyone, but it strikes me that to go through life with a name like Stenneth Flushpool, and then to marry Mrs Flushpool, is a most extraordinary run of bad luck!

Uncle Ralph left early after shaking my hand and giving me an electric shock with some infernal machine hidden in the palm of his hand.

Watched him disappear, a little round shape, wearing a little round crash helmet, perched on a little round scooter, and wondered if God loved him.

Hope so.

Only saw Gerald at church today. Out with Elsie somewhere or other the rest of the time. When he came in tonight, he waited till Anne went out of the room, then he said, 'Dad, I've got this great joke to tell you. Uncle Ralph told it me before he went this morning. It's about General Custer. You see, there was this man . . .'

'I've heard it!'

That joke's like a mosquito. I have to keep swatting it.

Monday March 10th

Wish Gerald and Anne wouldn't have these little private jokes together. This morning Gerald said 'How's your back, dad?'

'Fine,' I replied, 'never better. Must be the change in temperature. Why?'

Sniggers! Then Gerald said, 'Did you know that Ian Andrews is an anagram of 'Weird 'nanas'?'

'No,' I said. 'What's that got to do with it?'

Sniggers!

Edwin phoned this evening to ask if we could accommodate his little niece, Andromeda, for a few days, while her mum's in hospital. He added for some reason, that Andromeda's mum, Mrs Veal, is an ardent Christian feminist. Don't see what that's got to do with anything. Agreed to have the little girl, naturally. We love children, and, though I say it myself, I'm really rather good with them. Quite looking forward to it really.

Tuesday March 11th

Richard Cook round this evening. Brought young Charles with him, back for a couple of days from his second term at Deep Joy Bible School. What a difference from the miserable young man who came round that evening half way through January! Bit *too* much of a difference I thought. Kept looking at Anne and I with that I-can-see-right-through-you-because-I'm-ablaze-for-the-Lord expression you see on people's faces sometimes. Rather hoped Gerald wouldn't come in. He's in love and more flippant than ever. Charles was just in the middle of explaining to us how the holy spirit *really* operates, when Gerald came bouncing in.

'Hi, Charlie-boy,' he said, 'how are things down at the old Muppet factory?'

Anne and I glared, knowing how upset Richard gets sometimes, but Charles just looked very, very patient, and invited Gerald to a local meeting tomorrow night.

'I have a feeling,' said Charles meaningfully, 'that your needs will be mightily met there, Gerald.'

'Oh,' said Gerald, 'you mean they're having a bar?'

More patience from Charles, and a stern look from Richard. Gerald put his hands in the air and said, 'Alright, I give in, I give in! I'll come to the meeting!'

Hope it'll be alright. . . .

Wednesday March 12th

Andromeda Veal—age seven—has arrived!

Small but powerful. Conversation consists mainly of the phrase, 'I'm afraid I don't think that's very funny'. Clothes covered in obscure badges. Didn't like to ask what they all meant.

At bed-time I asked her if she'd brought any little dolly-friends along to go bye-byes with her. She called me a tool of the male sexist regime, and a false gender labeller. Thought this sounded a bit unsavoury, but was a little unsure of my ground, so didn't argue the point. What a cheek, though! Fumed inwardly as Anne wrestled her off to bed.

Wonder how Gerald's getting on at this meeting? He's a bit vulnerable at the moment, what with Elsie and . . . Elsie. Hope he's alright.

Thursday March 13th

Gerald very gloomy at breakfast. Says last night's speaker, someone called Bernard Brundle, has a special ministry to people who've somehow escaped feeling miserable and guilty. Now he feels *both*!

Andromeda spent most of the morning pointing out to Anne those aspects of our life-style that fall short of the socialist ideal. Anne reckons that when Jesus said we should all become like little children, he couldn't have met the Jewish equivalent of Andromeda Veal. Luckily, Andromeda adores Gerald's stereo headphone set. She's a bit confused though. Keeps referring to it as 'Gerald's personal problem'. Never mind. It keeps her occupied. Had to be almost nailed into bed again tonight. A tiring child!

Study-group led by 'my' convert, Ted, tonight.

Amazing! He's further on than I am. But then *he* hasn't got a family, has he?

Prayed for Kitty during the meeting. Apparently she's worse.

Friday March 14th

Gerald offered to settle Andromeda tonight before going to band practice. Said he'd got a plan. Absolute silence from upstairs after only a few minutes. Waited till Gerald came back down, then asked him what he'd done.

'Oh,' he said, 'I just told her that if she didn't go to sleep the bogey-person would get her. She's not frightened, just baffled.'

Still worried about Gerald. Very low since that meeting on Wednesday. Not like him at all.

Anne and I prayed for him and Kitty for quite a long time tonight.

Saturday March 15th

Really worried about Gerald now! Never seen him so miserable. When I got back from town today, he told me that Charles came round earlier to check he hadn't backslidden into happiness. He doesn't want to see Elsie this evening in case his gloom is infectious.

Met Andromeda on the stairs this afternoon. She asked me when I planned to release Anne from bondage, then stood outside the lavatory waiting for me to come out and give her an answer. I cannot *stand* people tutting and scuffing and sighing outside the lavatory when I'm *inside*!!

Terminated my stay somewhat prematurely, found Gerald's personal stereo, and stuck the headphones on Andromeda in mid-rhetoric.

Peace at last!

Bit of a surprise this evening. Edwin phoned, and happened to mention that tomorrow's guest speaker is Bernard Brundle, the man whose talk upset Gerald so much, earlier in the week! Didn't say anything to Edwin, but I'm a bit concerned. How's Gerald going to react to a second dose?

Sunday March 16th

To church with Anne, Gerald and Andromeda.

Told Gerald about Brundle, but he said he'd rather come to church and be made to feel guilty, rather than stay at home and feel even more guilty about not coming to church to feel guilty. *Think* I know what he meant.

Andromeda very watchful, and ominously quiet, during the first part of the service. Like sitting next to a small, slowly boiling, pig-tailed kettle.

I see what Gerald means about Brundle. Towards the end of his talk, he got an empty chair, set it in the middle in front of everybody, and looked round at us all in a here's-something-you-haven't-thought-of-before sort of way.

'Imagine if Jesus was sitting here in this chair right now,' he said. 'Wouldn't you feel bad? And wouldn't you just want to hide your face and creep away when you thought about all the things in your life that are not as they should be?'

Really did try to feel all those things, but I couldn't. Just felt excited about the idea of meeting

Jesus. Shows I've got an awful long way to go, I suppose.

At chorus time the little kettle boiled.

Andromeda stood up on her chair, stuck her chin out, and sang, 'SHE-E-E-E IS LO-O-ORD . . .', at the top of her voice. Raymond Pond, our organist, who's been very stable for a long time now, lost his head and launched into 'Home, home on the range'.

Wouldn't have mattered so much, but a few people started to sing the words with raised arms and passionately sincere expressions on their faces. Vernon Rawlings, completely carried away, shouted out, 'We want to be those Antelopes for *you*, Lord!'

Everything ground to a halt eventually. Andromeda triumphant. Gerald almost crying with laughter, Anne and I highly embarrassed.

Edwin came round this evening to collect Andromeda. Said not to worry—he knows his niece of old.

Relieved to see Gerald's spirits are quite restored. When we were all drinking cocoa tonight, he said, 'That chair *winked* at me this morning.'

Monday March 17th

Mrs Veal rang at *dawn*. Sounds like Andromeda cubed. She wanted to know why Andromeda was demanding a personal problem just like Gerald's.

Explained and laughed.

She said, 'I'm afraid I don't find that very funny,' and put the phone down.

Anne and I were very relieved to find a note on my pillow tonight from Gerald.

Dear Dad,
   Did you know that Selwyn
   Hughes is an anagram of
   Shye welsh gnu?
         Love, Gerald.

Back to normal. Thank you, God.

Tuesday March 18th

Spent yesterday evening enjoying the Veal-less atmosphere and reading a marvellous book called 'Two Thousand Things You Need To Know About Living The Victorious Christian Life'.

Written by Carlton S. Calhoun the third, who is, I believe, an American. Struck particularly by the section on giving. I see it all now! My motives for giving Mr Brain that money were all wrong. Paragraph 1,416 of the book says we must give cheerfully, without thought of reward or our own inconvenience. Explained this to Anne and Gerald at breakfast.

Gerald said, 'Can I have your bacon then?'

Anne said, 'There's a funny noise in the washing machine. Will you mend it for me?'

Why don't people take me seriously?

Wednesday March 19th

Edwin rang to ask if a small group could use our house on Saturday night to plan the Easter service. Agreed cheerfully and without etc etc. It works!

Anne mentioned the washing machine again. I said, 'Is it actually working, Anne?'

She said, 'Yes, but . . .'

Honestly! Women!

Thursday March 20th

Mildly interested to note that Gloria Marsh made another of her rare appearances at the study-group tonight. She mentioned casually at coffee-time that her car was going for repairs, so she would have transport problems for the next two days. I thought how incredible it was that on the one night when she comes, she should have a problem that I could help with. What a great opportunity to give without etc etc. Told her on the spot that she could have ours. Talk about surprised! Still protesting after I handed her the keys. Kissed me on the cheek. I think the poor helpless soul sees me as a sort of father figure.

Suddenly saw Anne glaring at me through the hatch. Must show her that book. She doesn't seem to understand giving.

Friday March 21st

Cold atmosphere at breakfast. Asked Anne why she wasn't speaking.

She said, 'I'm saving my energy for when I *walk* into town later.'

Told her what Mr Calhoun says about giving without etc etc.

She said, 'Yes, but you're giving without thought of *my* inconvenience, not yours! She only came last night because of the car, and now she's got it!'

Appalled by this uncharitable assessment of Gloria. I intend to remain cheerful about it, whatever happens.

Saturday March 22nd

Things still very cool. Suddenly remembered I'd forgotten to tell Anne about the meeting here tonight. Tried to get Gerald to tell her, but he wouldn't. Eventually told her through the hatch.

She said, 'Actually, it doesn't matter, because we can't go out anywhere much without the car today, so I'll just stay in here all day, and make food for this evening.'

Heard Gerald singing 'Fight the Good Fight' somewhere upstairs. Very funny—I don't think!

Meeting started at 7.30 p.m. There was Edwin, Leonard Thynn, Richard Cook and George Farmer.

Gerald asked if he could stay for a minute because he had an idea. Someone was silly enough to say he could.

Gerald said, 'Right! Here's my idea for the Easter service. What we do is, we run a wire from one end of the church to the other, and just before the service ends, we slide an enormous artificial chicken along over people's heads, then when it gets to the middle it lays a great big egg into the centre aisle, and when it lands it cracks open, and—this is the *really* good bit—Richard's inside, dressed in a fluffy yellow chick costume and he stands up and shouts 'New Life!' Then we release twenty or thirty live chickens into the congregation just to make it a real *experience* for everybody. What do you think?'

Smiles all round except for Richard, frozen in a listening position, sausage roll poised uneaten in front of his open mouth. Thought Gerald might've gone too far this time. Richard slowly grounded his sausage roll, then looked up very gravely at Gerald. He said, 'Where would we get the chickens from?'

Stupid Thynn showered us all with puff-pastry at this point. Had to be patted on the back and given sips of water.

I'll kill Gerald one of these days!

Good meeting after that. *I'm* to do a testimony in the Easter Sunday service.

Car still not back. Anne tight-lipped. Never mind. Surely Gloria will bring it back in the morning. I'm still cheerful!

Sunday March 23rd

Felt uncomfortable at church today. Don't know why. Couldn't even smile when George Farmer said he wanted to hear a spontaneous burst of applause after the next chorus.

On the way home our car passed us, full of Gloria and several men, all singing and laughing. Some of them seemed to be holding bottles.

Anne said, 'Look, the poor helpless soul has organised some sort of charity outing.'

Car still not back tonight. Read Mr Calhoun's advice again and took courage. Who am I to judge?

Anne said 'Washing machine' in her sleep.

Monday March 24th

Car not back.

Tuesday March 25th

Car not back. Civil war imminent. Anne says go round and ask her what she thinks she's doing. Can't. I'm chicken. Prayed instead.

Wednesday March 26th

I WANT MY CAR BACK!!!

If that idiot Calhoun was here, I'd send him round to Gloria's to get it, then I'd give him a right hook cheerfully and without thought of reward or inconvenience to myself.

Thursday March 27th

10.00 a.m.

I'm supposed to be giving a Christian testimony in three days time, and I hate everybody I meet!

WHERE'S MY BLOODY CAR?!?!

6.00 p.m.

Gloria at the door. She'd brought the car back. Said her car had taken a teensy-weensy bit longer to repair than she'd expected, and she hoped I didn't mind. Also she'd had the itsy-bitsiest little bump you ever saw with another horrid car, and there was a titchy little mark on one of the wings. But she was *so* grateful, especially as, on Sunday, she had been able to take out a couple of dear friends who weren't able to get about much these days and it was all because I'd been such a dream-lover about the car.

Cleared my throat loudly to cover Anne's snort from the kitchen.

Went and looked at the car when she'd gone.

It was crouching miserably by the kerb, looking exhausted and reproachful. The titchy mark was a huge dent. Anne and Gerald came out too.

Anne said, 'She's bent it.'

Gerald said, 'Dolly Parton's suckered you, Dad.'

Too fed up to even tell him off.

After study-group, spent two hours staring at a blank sheet of paper. Testimony? Me? Huh!!!

Friday March 28th

Good Friday.

Anne's being very nice but I just feel stupid and useless. Praying's like shouting into a concrete bucket. I'll never be ready for Easter. Terrified about this testimony. I'll have to make it up.

No-one ever felt like I do tonight.

(N.B. Must have a look at that washing machine.)

Saturday March 29th

9.00 a.m.

Rang Edwin. Said couldn't he ask someone on a spiritual high to give a testimony instead of me. He said, gently but firmly, 'You do it. Just talk about where you are. Be honest.'

I'm dreading it.

(Nearly looked at washing machine. Couldn't face it in the end.)

10.30 a.m.

Who should ring but Gloria Marsh! Could she speak to Anne? When she came back through, Anne said, 'Gloria's got to go into hospital unexpectedly in the next hour. She's terrified. She asked if I would go with her and look after her.'

I said, 'I bet you gave her a short answer to that!'

'I did,' said Anne. 'I said "Yes". I'm off straightaway. Back after tea sometime.'

Couldn't believe my ears.

'But what about the pictures with Brenda Rawlings this afternoon,' I said. 'You've been looking forward to it for weeks. And what about all that business with the car? You said that . . .'

Anne smiled at me in a funny way she does sometimes. Came over and kissed me. She said, 'Darling, go and read paragraph 1,416 again.'

I did.

Got some flowers to send to Gloria.

Wrote my testimony.

Played Scrabble with Gerald. He won by using naughty words.

Sunday March 30th

Easter Day!!

Thanked God quietly at church for Jesus and Anne. Did more or less the same in my testimony. Felt odd telling the truth in church. Good though! So happy I nearly danced. (Only nearly!)

Monday March 31st

First really happy breakfast for some time. Gerald announced that my name is an anagram of 'Sprain salad'. We all laughed.

Good quiet-time. I shall never get low again!

Tuesday April 1st

8.30 a.m.

Gerald must think I'm stupid!

Knowing he has a friend living in Northern Italy, I calmly laid aside a letter from Rome, inviting me to take up the post of Deputy Pope, and promising a salary of one million lire per week, with as much fish as I could eat. I shall walk to work now, comfortable in the knowledge that I have emerged unscathed from my son's annual attempt to make an idiot of me.

9.15 a.m.

Three people came up from behind me on my way to work, looked into my face, laughed, and shook my hand. Looked in the mirror when I got to work and found a big notice stuck to my back. It said,

'IF THIS MAN'S FACE REMINDS YOU OF A DISAPPOINTED CAMEL, PLEASE SHAKE HIS HAND.'

118

Sometimes I think Gerald's sense of humour needs pruning!

Wednesday April 2nd

Enjoyed quiet-time again this morning. Life felt perfect. Couldn't imagine anything going wrong.
8.30 p.m.

Everything's gone wrong!

The Flushpools appeared at the door this evening. Sat in a row of two on our sofa. Said they'd felt led to come round after hearing my testimony.

I said, 'What about my testimony?'

Mrs Flushpool said, 'You shared with us that your marriage had moved into Satan's camp for a season.'

I said, 'I don't remember saying that.'

Anne said, 'She means that you said we'd had a few rows lately.'

Mrs Flushpool didn't seem to hear. She said, 'The Lord would have us ask you if there are physical problems in your union. We have a special ministry to those with . . . physical problems in their union.'

Completely mystified. Told them I don't belong to a union.

He said, 'We speak carnally, brother.'

To my surprise Anne suddenly got up and said, 'I'm awfully sorry, Mr and Mrs Flushpool, I don't think we can help you. There must be people around with problems like that, though. I'm sure you'll find somebody. Good evening. Why don't you see them to the door, darling?'

Sometimes I honestly wonder if I'm a bit slow on the uptake. Found myself at the door saying goodbye to the Flushpools, without really knowing what had been going on. Mrs F. seemed almost angry for some reason. But she smiled sweetly at me as she went out, then stopped on the doorstep and said, 'Can I say something to you in love, dear brother Adrian?'

Thought—oh, no! Said 'Yes. Please do.'

She said, 'Of course, your testimony wasn't really a testimony, was it? Descriptions of the way in which you have failed The Lord can hardly be said to glorify God, can they? I do hope things are soon better between you and *dear* Anne. Goodnight, dear, and God bless you.'

Felt very uneasy after they'd gone. Maybe she was right. Was I *too* honest? I think I probably was . . .

Thursday April 3rd

She *was* right! I let God down on Sunday.

Friday April 4th

No-one's ever felt as bad as I feel tonight.
Anne and Gerald haven't noticed! Why not?

Saturday April 5th

Easter seems so far away now. Feeling really low. What use is a twit like me to God?

Wasted an entire evening looking miserable but bravely cheerful. At last Anne said, 'Are you alright, darling?'

'Oh, yes,' I lied heroically, 'I'm fine; you don't have to worry about me.'

'Thank goodness for that!' she said. 'I'm off to bed.'

Fancy believing me!!!

Sunday April 6th

Gerald arrived bleary-eyed but quietly content at the breakfast table. Announced that Graham Kendrick is an anagram of 'Grandmah Kicker'. Anne laughed like a drain. I produced a rather good shuddering sigh.

They didn't even notice!!

Good job I'm not the self-pitying type.

To church.

Why is George Farmer allowed to lead services? Told us to look around as we sang choruses, expressing Christian love to any brother or sister who caught our eye.

Groaned inwardly.

Stared fixedly at the overhead-projector screen, screwing my eyes up to look as if I didn't know the words well enough to look away. Glancing aside in an unguarded moment, I was impaled by a sisterly beam from pretty Norma Twill. Tried to smile back in a brotherly, going-on-well-with-the-Lord sort of way, but a muscle in my face just refused to work. The side of my mouth dropped open in a horrible leer, and one eye began winking uncontrollably. Norma turned pale, then looked compassionate. Went all hot as I realised she was remembering my so-called 'lust problem', back in December!

Afterwards, at coffee-time, I said, 'Sorry, Norma, a muscle in my face got stuck.'

She fell about laughing.

Later, at home, I told Anne, Gerald, and Leonard Thynn (who'd come to borrow the cat for some insane reason) about Norma. I sometimes think I'm just a one-man comedy show. They were all in hysterics!

Monday April 7th

Still low.

Quiet-time *too* quiet.

Prayed for an encouraging sign. Suddenly the door-bell rang. Rushed downstairs quite excited. It was Leonard Thynn returning the stupid cat.

Tuesday April 8th

God's on holiday. . . .

(Why borrow a *cat*?)

Wednesday April 9th

Edwin phoned to confirm that the study-group could meet here tomorrow night. I suppose that's all I'm good for—providing a house for others to be spiritual in!

(A cat???)

Thursday April 10th

Study-group began as usual about eight o'clock. Deliberately sat on the floor near the door, so that I could escape easily if I had to.

Started with a discussion on euthanasia. Deaf old Mrs Thynn shocked everyone by saying that she thought it was absolutely lovely, and she'd like her grandchildren to have a chance to sit and watch it from beginning to end!

Stunned silence until Anne suddenly giggled, and said, 'She thinks it's a Walt Disney film.' General atmosphere of relief, except from Richard Cook, who'd obviously been about to fire several rounds of scripture from the hip.

Discussion droned on.

Kept my eyes open during the prayer time. Everyone else locked in the 'shampoo position', as Gerald calls it. Wondered how many were sincere. Decided not many.

Edwin stayed on afterwards. Said he wanted a 'chat'. Felt a little nervous. Edwin *knows* things sometimes.

'Cheer up!' said Edwin, 'I've got a little job to offer you.'

Panic!!! 'What err . . . job's that then, Edwin?'

'Well, I think—I'm not absolutely sure, mind—but I *think* the Lord wants you to be a study-group leader.'

Started babbling about being bad and useless and not clever enough. Edwin interrupted me.

'It was during your testimony at Easter that the idea first came into my head. I was very impressed with how honest you were. Helped a lot of people, you know.'

Started to say something, but he held up his hand to stop me.

'Don't give me an answer now. Think about it. Let me know tomorrow. Ask *Him*.

11.45

Prayed in bed with Anne just now.

She said, 'I think Edwin's right.'

I like Anne being sure. 'Yes,' I said, 'so do I.'

Sat for a while, thinking/worrying/feeling pleased. Suddenly remembered what I'd meant to ask Anne.

'Anne, why did Leonard want to borrow the . . . ?'

She was fast asleep.

1.30 a.m.

Still awake. Hope my group don't go all quiet. Hope George Farmer's one of my group. He'll keep 'em on their toes. . . .

Friday April 11th

Rang Edwin first thing this morning to tell him my decision. Sounded very pleased. Told Gerald at breakfast. He *didn't* make a joke!

I am a study-group leader!

I *am* a study-group leader!!

I am *a* study-group leader!!!

I am a *study-group* leader!!!!

I am a study-group *leader*!!!!!

Thanked God in my quiet-time that I am not a proud man. Can't help feeling a new sense of importance, though. *Me!* A study-group leader! Well, well!

Saturday April 12th

Ridiculous incident this morning, just as I was enjoying my new sensation of deep, spiritual dignity. Busy washing up and thinking about my first study-group as a leader, this Thursday, when I put my hand into the washing-up bowl and cut my thumb quite badly on the bread knife. Started to bleed quite heavily.

Gerald, who was drying up said, 'How did you do that, dad?'

'Like this,' I said, and put my other hand in the washing-up bowl. Cut my other thumb. Ended up with an absurd, white bulbous bandage on *both* thumbs.

Anne and Gerald both very sympathetic, but had

to take turns going out of the room to laugh. How embarrassing!

Bet Billy Graham never had to face his public with two bulging bandaged thumbs. Bit of an early setback really. Can't help feeling nervous about church

tomorrow. I know what'll happen—Leonard Thynn will just cackle, Doreen Cook will want to lay hands on my thumbs, and everyone else will be very compassionate and secretly want to ask me how on earth I could've injured *both* thumbs!

Sunday April 13th

What a relief. Edwin rang early to say that there's no church this morning. Gave me a list of names (*my* study-group!) to phone and pass on the news to. Asked him why church was off. He said, 'Oh there was a mix-up in the bookings for Unity Hall. Nobody's fault really, but the local cage-bird society have got it for the morning.'

When I told Gerald about this, he said, 'Oh, it'll be business as usual up at the old hall this morning, then.'

Now that I have a position of responsibility in the church, I don't intend to allow this kind of foolish comment from Gerald. Gave him a look that was supposed to combine fundamental acceptance with loving but firm chastisement.

Gerald said, 'Thumbs giving you stick, eh, Dad?'

Went off to meet Elsie before I could put him straight.

Decided this afternoon that, as a study-group leader, a dramatic improvement is needed in my prayer-life. Intend to pray for two solid hours *every* night after Anne's gone to bed. Two hours should be enough—don't want to overdo it.

1.30 a.m.

So far so good. Prayed from 11.15 until 1.15. Feel tired but mystical. Must keep it up.

Monday April 14th

Rather a shame Anne and Gerald can't make the same efforts over consideration for others as I'm making over prayer. The row they made getting up

126

this morning when I was trying to get a bit of extra sleep!

Forgave them.

Seven separate people at work asked how I 'did my thumbs'. Everett Glander made what can only be described as an unsavoury suggestion about the cause of my injuries. If I wasn't a Christian and a study-group leader I'd push Glander's head through the shredder.

Hope these bandages are off by Thursday!!

About to start my new extra prayer-time this evening, but got distracted by the quarter-finals of the North-East Bedfordshire indoor bowls championship on TV. Suddenly it's 1.00 a.m.! Too tired to pray. Why have I watched bowls instead of praying? I don't *play* bowls! I'm not *interested* in bowls!

Never mind—tomorrow, I'll get it *right*.

Tuesday April 15th

6.00 p.m.

Overheard Gerald on the phone when I got home just now.

'. . . and then, Elsie—*then*, he put the *other* hand in, and—oh! Hello Dad . . .'

If the Bible's right about long life depending on respect for parents, Gerald will be lucky to make it to Saturday, let alone three score years and ten.

2.00 a.m.

Really, truly, honestly, *did* intend to pray tonight. Got caught up in a long Albanian film with sub-titles, set in a kitchen. Kept thinking something was going to happen, but it never did, and suddenly the film finished.

Have crawled to bed. . . .

Wednesday April 16th

Felt exhausted and morose at breakfast.

Anne said, 'How's the late prayer going, darling?'

Couldn't meet her eye. 'Alright,' I mumbled.

Gerald said, 'Were you speaking in tongues most of the time, dad? I could have sworn I heard you speaking in Albanian for ages.'

Very funny! Deliberately didn't smile later on when he asked if I knew that David Owen was an anagram of 'An odd view'.

Fell asleep at work today.

Leonard Thynn came round this evening while I was asleep in my chair after supper. He drew little faces on my thumb bandages with felt-pen and wrote 'Thynn was here' underneath, on both of them. Anne and Gerald just let him! They were all sitting with foolish grins on their faces when I woke up. Thynn can be very silly sometimes. Suggested *all* the members of our study-group should wear bandages on their thumbs, like a secret society. Gerald suggested our theme tune should be 'Thumb enchanted evening'. Thynn cackled at this, then said he knew a way to cope with problems such as my thumbs. Asked wearily what it was. He told me to go and stand behind the television. Decided to humour him. Stood behind the TV and said, 'Alright, Leonard, how does this help?'

'Well,' said Leonard, 'it teaches you how to face set-backs!'

They all roared.

Forgave them.

Thursday April 17th

Was absolutely determined to get the prayer thing right last night. Knelt down at 11.00 p.m. and closed my eyes. Woken and manhandled to bed at 4.00 a.m. by Anne. Didn't seem over-sympathetic really.

Fell asleep at work again. Glander poured ice-cold water on me, then claimed to have raised me from the dead when I sat up at my desk and shrieked.

So tired!!

Got home to find Anne with one of those okay-this-is-going-to-get-sorted-out-right-now expressions on her face.

She said, 'Darling, tell me why you can't go to bed early and then get up early to pray.'

'Oh,' I said, 'I don't like getting up . . .'

'Quite!' said Anne. 'And I don't like being joined every morning by a guilty, exhausted, disillusioned mystic. Besides . . .'

She smiled shyly.

'I . . . well, I miss you at night. Couldn't you just *try* the other way? Just for a while?'

Promised I'd try.

10.00 p.m.

My first meeting as a study-group leader is over.

Not a particularly good start to the evening. Apart from feeling exhausted and still wearing my ridiculous bandages, the members of the group seemed to have undergone a mysterious change since last week. Last time we met most of them were pleasant, easy-going people who co-operated with group aims. This week they were awkward, late, (some of them) difficult to quieten down when it was time to start, and generally unresponsive.

Really wanted to throttle Thynn, who does tend to

wear a joke out. He went up to each person as they came in, and sang 'Thumbwhere, over the rainbow . . .' and pointed at me with a stupid smirk on his face.

Wondered why I'd not noticed before what a rebellious crowd of people these are. When we got going at last, I noted that Norma Twill was insufficiently joyful during the choruses, Vernon Rawlings yawned in the middle of the scripture reading, and Percy Brain had his eyes open during the prayers.

Profound silence for an hour and a half as I delivered a study on 'The function of fruit in the Old Testament'. Asked if there were any questions at the end. Long, rather disappointing silence, until young Bessie Trench raised her hand.

'Yes, Bessie?' I said, 'What's your question?'

Really pleased someone had been listening.

Bessie twisted her fingers together and cleared her throat.

She said, 'How did you do your thumbs?'

10.15 p.m.

Going to bed now. Seems ridiculously early, still . . .

Friday April 18th

9.00 a.m.

Up at 6.00 a.m.! Good prayer-time. Glad I decided to switch to the morning. Asked Anne at breakfast why she thought people were deliberately making things difficult for me now that I'm a study-group leader.

She laughed!

'It's not *them* that have changed, darling. It's you! You're a leader now. It's just that all their funny little ways didn't bother you before. Now you notice everything, and you think it's something to do with how they feel about you. They're not there to make *you* feel better, you know; you're supposed to be serving *them*, not the other way round.'

Yes . . . well . . . perhaps . . .

Bandages off my thumbs before going to work this morning, thank goodness. No more silly comments. Great!

6.00 p.m.

Small boy stopped me on the way home from work just now . . .

'Oi, mister! ow come yer fumbs is all white 'n' crinkly, an' the rest of yer 'ands ain't?'

(Don't dare ring Bill Dove to ask about Kitty at the moment.)

Saturday April 19th

Anne and Gerald off early in the car to visit Mick and Samantha Rind-Smythe who used to live in Frank Braddock's house. I can't go because of work. Just before going, Anne said, 'Whatever you do, don't forget to feed the rabbit, and if you could just take a look at the washing machine—it really is getting worse. The rabbit's the main thing though. You *won't* forget it will you?'

Really—you'd think I was a complete idiot! I may not have had much to do with Brenda, our rabbit (Anne usually feeds her), but I'm not likely to forget to feed her.

Leonard Thynn's looking after the cat. Anne says he's borrowed it again. Must remember to ask her why. . . .

Forgot to feed the rabbit yesterday. Old Miss Seed, whose garden backs on to the end of ours, came to the door early this morning, carrying Brenda, who'd escaped from the hutch and spent the night eating

Miss Seed's 'treasured' plants. Miss Seed rather annoyed but quite nice about it really. Promised to reinforce the hutch. Patched it up a bit.

To church.

Very challenging talk from Edwin today. Short (two fruit-gums) but good. Said we should all be aware of chances to witness to our immediate neighbours. Percy Brain and Frank Braddock are already Christians, so that just left Miss Seed, who we've hardly ever spoken to. Thought how amazing it was that this 'rabbit' connection had happened earlier. Decided to contact Miss Seed after lunch.

Got home from church. Saw Brenda from an upstairs window, sitting in Miss Seed's flower bed, stuffing herself with more plants. Crept along under the hedge at the end of our garden, rattling food in a bowl and whispering, 'Come back, Brenda! I have dominion over you!'

Brenda can't have read that scripture.

Hid indoors, but had to answer the door after repeated knocking. Miss Seed with a scratch down one arm and Brenda under the other. Rather cool this time. I babbled apologies foolishly. 'Won't happen again . . . etc etc.' Not the moment for evangelism really. . . .

Can't do any more with the hutch until the shops open tomorrow. Have put Brenda in the house for the time being. It'll be alright as long as I keep the front and back doors shut!

Monday April 21st

10.00 a.m. At work.

Went out the back after prayer-time this morning to check what I needed for the hutch. There'll be no mistake about it *this* time! Closed the front door very carefully behind me as I left for work. I'll get wire-netting and staples on the way home, and that'll be the end of the problem.

10.00 p.m.

Got home from work to find that I'd left the *back* door open. Rushed round the house, hoping against hope that Brenda was still there somewhere. Lots of little round black pellets, but no rabbit. Spotted her eventually through the hedge, chewing smugly at me, with bits of Miss Seed's plants sticking out of the sides of her mouth, and her stupid great ears sticking up like two black exclamation marks.

Nearly fainted at the prospect of facing Miss Seed again. Prayed for the Second Coming. No luck. Phone went. It was Miss Seed. Said she realised it might be a little upsetting for me, but she didn't intend to spend the rest of her life cultivating food for my rabbit. Would I collect it—at once! Got Brenda back after a long undignified chase punctuated by a series of unsuccessful flying leaps. Shoved her hutch right up against the brick wall in the yard, and stapled two layers of thick wire-netting over the rest of it. Brenda sat inside chewing over ideas like a little one-rabbit escape committee. She won't get out this time, though! Secure at last! Life was beginning to seem only about great big black rabbits.

Tuesday April 22nd

10.00 a.m. At work.

Woke feeling peaceful for once. Off to work in a relaxed frame of mind. I can give a bit more thought to my study-group now that I don't have to worry about the rabbit. Also, I've forgotten that originally, I was planning to witness to Miss Seed, and I haven't. As soon as I get home, I'll ring her.

7.30 p.m.

Rang Miss Seed shortly after getting home. I said, 'Miss Seed, there's something I want to share with you.'

'Other than your rabbit, you mean?' she said icily.

Went all hot and cold.

'You mean . . . you don't mean . . . ?'

'Yes, Mr Plass! I *do* mean.'

Realised to my horror, that Brenda, wearing whatever Super-rabbit costume she dons when nobody's looking, must have squeezed between the hutch and the wall, and sprinted triumphantly down to eat Miss Seed's succulent vegetation again.

'I'll nail the hutch to the wall,' I promised wildly.

'Why don't you nail the rabbit to the wall?' suggested Miss Seed acidly.

Took over an hour catching Brenda. When I arrived in Miss Seed's garden, she hopped through the hedge into our's. Rushed back round to our's just in time to see her disappear through the hedge into Miss Seed's. Rushed round . . . etc etc. I swear that animal grinned at me with her two big white front teeth, as I lurched wearily after her each time. Got home exhausted, and deeply anti-rabbit.

Nailed her hutch to the wall.

Wednesday April 23rd

Bad dreams all night about being chased by a huge rabbit which changed into Richard Cook just as it caught me, and said, 'Feed me! Feed me!'

Woke at 5.00 a.m. Checked Brenda every fifteen minutes from 5.15 onwards. No work today. By the time Anne and Gerald came back I was a nervous wreck. Told Anne all about the rabbit, then slumped down in an easy chair while she went out to put the kettle on. Everything seems much calmer and safer when Anne's here.

Bit later, Gerald came in and said, 'Cor, Dad! You've really boxed the old rabbit in, haven't you?'

Nodded wearily.

'I've let her out for a little hop-about,' said Gerald, 'just to . . .'

Launched myself at his throat with a wild strangled cry. 'You what . . . ?!!!'

'Only joking, Dad! Only joking . . . Mum told me all about it . . .'

Didn't kill him.

Rang Miss Seed after talking to Anne. Anne said to make friends first, *then* think about witnessing.

'Don't judge me on my rabbit retention record, Miss Seed,' I pleaded on the phone.

'As long as you don't judge *me* on my rabbit rejection record,' she responded.

We laughed and arranged coffee tomorrow.

Later, Gerald said, 'You remember when you went out with Leonard, dad, the night you met Ted?'

'Yes,' I said, 'what about it?'

'Well, you remember I said that witnessing as an anagram of 'sing in stew'?'

'Yes, so . . . ?'

'Well, I forgot to mention something at the time.'

'What?'

'It's *rabbit* stew.'

Thursday April 24th

Spent part of my prayer-time this morning thinking about what Anne said on Friday. She's absolutely right! My job is to serve the study-group, not tell them what to do and judge them. After all, look at me and the rabbit. 'Let he who is without rabbits . . . etc'

No . . . from now on I'm going to put myself entirely at the disposal of the members of my study-group, ready and willing to pour myself out for them in every way that's necessary. Hallelujah! Oddly enough, when I expressed all this to Anne, she looked a bit worried. Perhaps when one takes a spiritual step forward (albeit very humbly), as I feel I've done, it's bound to threaten others a little.

Have decided to give a duplicated letter to each of the people in my group tonight offering my services as a Christian friend and counsellor at any time of the day or night. Spent the time between getting home from work and study-group, getting the letter ready and planning the meeting. Afraid I had to speak a little sharply to Anne once or twice. She's still fretting about the washing machine and odd bits of rabbit dung that got trodden in the other day. I feel that the Lord would not have me troubled with these things at this time.

10.00 p.m.

What an amazing meeting! We were all mightily blessed! (Thynn says he wasn't, but I told him he was in ways that he knows not of.)

My letter received with great enthusiasm. Amazed to find one or two people approached me *this evening* with problems that will need dealing with in the next few days!

There is a world of need! I hear the call! I am ready!

Friday April 25th

Out. New washer: Norma Twill.

Saturday April 26th

Out again. Percy Brain: Doubt.

Sunday April 27th

Church.
Out: Norman Simmonds—Furniture moving
 ,, : Norma Twill—check washer
 ,, : Deaf old Mrs Thynn—Explained that old Mr Verge next-door (who she hit with one of Leonard's Doc Martin ten-holers) said he wanted to '*speak* with her', not '*sleep* with her'.

Monday April 28th

Out. Vernon Rawlings: Lust and allied problems.

Tuesday April 29th

Out. Study-group leaders' meeting: (I'm one)

Wednesday April 30th

Out. Stenneth Flushpool: Dominoes while Mrs F. was out. Very excited. (Him I mean)

Thursday May 1st

Out before study-group. Ephraim Trench: Pregnant cow. (Rang me by mistake instead of the vet)

Great study-group. Planning/talking about the Lord's work. Reminded everybody that I'm always available.

Friday May 2nd

Out. George Farmer: Prayer re fruit.

Have had to cut morning prayer right down to save energy for church work in evenings.

Saturday May 3rd

Out. Norma Twill: Double check washer.

Sunday May 4th

Church.
Out.

Monday May 5th

Out.

Tuesday May 6th

Out.

Wednesday May 7th

Out.

Thursday May 8th

Out—study-group—out.

Friday May 9th

Out.

Saturday May 10th

First time I've had the chance to write much in my diary for a while. Life is good! Being a study-group leader is a real privilege. Never felt so humble. Constantly busy with pastoral work. Hallelujah!

Sorry to say Anne and Gerald are not totally supportive. Anne seems obsessed by this fault in the washing machine. Can anything be of more importance than the Lord's work?

As for Gerald—if he says 'Keep your hair on, Moses' one more time, there'll be trouble.

Sunday May 11th

To church. Can't understand people who don't join in at church. I really question their commitment. Makes life so difficult for us leaders. Gerald didn't come today. Said he was suffering from a pain in the neck, and wanted a rest from it. Odd way of putting it!

Anne asked about the washing machine again this evening. Suddenly remembered Percy Brain's ear ache. Felt led to pop round and pray with him. Stayed late, listening to Percy's theatrical stories. Hilarious! Left, feeling I'd really brought joy into the old boy's lonely life. Home at midnight to find Anne hand washing clothes in the sink.

I said, 'Anne, love, scripture teaches the body is the temple of the holy spirit. Shouldn't this have been done earlier?'

No reply, but something about her back showed she was really listening. Straight to bed. Asleep in seconds.

Monday May 12th

Decorated the Thynn's hall tonight with Leonard. Stayed for Scrabble afterwards. Felt right, as it's a very relationship-building activity.

Back late to find a note from Gerald saying that Roger Forster is an anagram of 'Frog restorer'. Tore it up. I will not tolerate disrespect in this house!

Tuesday May 13th

About to tackle washing machine when the phone rang. It was young Vernon Rawlings asking what passage we would be studying on Thursday. Dropped everything and said I'd be round immediately to explain.

Anne looked furious. Funny—I thought she liked young Vernon.

Wednesday May 14th

Really annoyed! Gerald's tinkered with the washing machine and made it worse. Reminded him that scripture says we must be good stewards and not go round causing extra expense by meddling.

A little later, as I was leaving to help the Cooks with young Charles' problem about free will and predestination, I distinctly heard Anne and Gerald arguing in the log shed about who should use the axe first. Curious!

Thursday May 15th

Are Anne and Gerald undergoing a spiritual crisis? I have discerned that their general attitude is cold and unresponsive. Neither of them said anything at the study-group tonight.

Later, while she was washing-up the coffee cups, I said to Anne, 'Anne, I think I've got a word for you.'

She said, 'And I've got one for you if that machine's not soon fixed!'

Prayed for her.

Friday May 16th

6.15

Home at six to find everyone out and a note on the side from Anne, alerting me to the fact that an abandoned family has turned up in Humph's cafe, just round the corner from us. Could I deal with it? Great! Spiritual adventure! I feel like the Red Adaire of the Christian world. I shall go out now, armed with the Spirit and the Word, to face and do battle with whatever forces of darkness await me!

8.30 p.m.

Got round to Humph's cafe about 6.30, but apart from Humph, the only people in there were Anne and Gerald! They were sitting by a table right at the back, drinking tea. Couldn't think what was going on. Sat down at the table with them. I said 'Where's the abandoned family?'

Gerald said, 'We're it.'

'But it was just . . . I was just . . . just doing the Lord's work . . .'

Anne said, 'We thought perhaps *we* might be the Lord's work as well—just now and then, if that's alright?'

Gerald bought chips all round. I promised to mend the washing machine. I said sorry. We all laughed. We reckoned God laughed too.

Saturday May 17th

Mended the washing machine this morning. Took seven minutes. Went for a walk with Anne afterwards. She tells me the 'abandoned family' was Frank Braddock's idea. Also said Frank told her he was at school with Father John, hence the Bungles/Smelly business. Both converted on the same day apparently. Ended up different but the same—funny really.

Feel as if I've woken up after a long feverish dream today. Rang Leonard after lunch and asked him what he'd give me out of ten for my performance as a study-group leader so far.

He said, 'Absolutely *no* doubt about that. Ten out of ten! Easily!'

I said, 'How many if you tell the truth?'

'Minus three,' said Thynn.

Thanked him for telling the truth and said things would be changing now. Just about to put the phone down when I remembered something.

'Leonard, why did you borrow the . . .'

He'd put the 'phone down.

Sunday May 18th

About to set off for church this morning, when the phone went. Almost left it, but decided it might be important. It was Bill Dove.

'Just wanted to tell yer,' he said quietly, 'that Kitty's gone. Six o'clock this mornin'. She smiled that little smile of 'ers and said, "Time's up, love, see yer later", and that was it.'

Couldn't speak.

'She gave me a message for you last night,' went on Bill. 'Made me promise to pass it on soon as she'd gone.'

Could barely manage a whisper. 'What did she say?'

'She said, "Tell 'im, Bill, that Kitty said God loves 'im more than she does, so everythin's gotter be alright."'

'Thanks Bill . . . thanks . . . Is there anything I can . . . ?'

'Nothin' just now,' said Bill. 'See yer, mate.'

Told Anne and Gerald. We put our arms round each other for a little while, then went to church.

She always made me feel good.

Monday May 19th

Reminded by Anne this morning that it's only six days until we set off for our annual trip to 'Let God Spring into Royal Acts of Harvest Growth', the big Christian festival down at Wetbridge in the Westcountry. A whole group of us are going from the church. Rather looking forward to it this year. Other year's we've rented caravans. This year we've bought a tent! Can't wait! Bacon sizzling deliciously on the primus every morning—the healthy feel of open-air living—soft talk under the stars each evening—good fellowship with other campers and caravanners— marvellous! Roll on Saturday!

I've insisted that we leave *very* early, probably about 4.00 a.m. Gerald groaned and Anne sighed when I said this, but it's the *only* way to do it. Up with the lark!

This evening Gerald said, 'Are you sure your back will be okay for camping, dad? Might be a bit cold down at Wetbridge.'

I said, 'Should be alright—I haven't felt so much as a twinge since . . . ooh, must be February or March—touch wood.'

Why does my back make Anne and Gerald laugh?

Tuesday May 20th

Rather embarrassed this evening. Edwin, Richard, Percy Brain and Leonard came round for the evening. After a bit Leonard said, 'What's the silliest thing each of us has ever done?'

Quite amusing after that, until it got to Gerald's turn. Instead of talking about the silliest thing *he'd* ever done, he reeled off a long list of the silliest things *I've* ever done. Edwin and Percy were in fits! When Gerald described how he and Anne had found me lying in the hall with my feet up against the door, I thought Edwin was going to do himself an injury, and when he got onto me shouting at a paper-clip, Thynn *did* do himself an injury. He was lying on the floor, on his front, weeping with laughter, and banging the carpet with his fist, when he accidentally punched himself on the nose. I was pleased. Gerald was just about to get on to the 'Hot thighs in wet grass' saga, when Anne came in carrying a suit on a hanger in one hand, and a piece of paper in the other. Felt very glad she'd interrupted.

'We're just talking about one or two of Dad's sillier moments, Mum,' said Gerald.

'Vastly entertaining!' chuckled Percy.

Thynn still prostrate, heaving weakly from time to time. Edwin smiling and shaking his head.

Saw Anne glance at the paper in her hand.

She said, 'Oh, well, I won't interrupt. It's just that your suit's back from the cleaners and there's a note . . . I'll come back later.'

Didn't want to get back to 'Hot thighs in wet grass'! I said, 'It's perfectly alright, Anne, carry on—there's a note, you said? A note about what?'

'I don't think . . .'

I said, 'Look, Anne, we weren't talking about anything important, just some silly incidents that have perfectly rational explanations. Please go on, Anne.'

'I don't . . .'

'Please, Anne!'

'It's just that the cleaners found a note in your pocket before they cleaned the suit, and I wondered . . . I'll come back later.'

'Anne, please read the note! What's the matter with you?'

'I don't . . .'

'Anne!!'

'Well, alright . . . if you say so. The . . . the note's in your handwriting, and it says . . . I'll come back later . . .'

'Anne!!!'

'It says "Buy a tree-frog and call it Kaiser Bill".'

Unable to provide the perfectly rational explanation for my memo-to-self, because no-one would listen. All helpless and collapsing with laughter— even Richard, braying like a donkey.

Reminded Anne and Gerald tonight that we're leaving at *four* on Saturday. I know them. They think I'll forget.

Wednesday May 21st

Prayer time's settled down to an hour each morning now. Just right. Having to fend off some of the visiting requests from my study-group. All my own fault of course, but really! Raymond Pond wanted me to come round and feed his gerbil this evening. When I asked why, he said he was nicely settled by the fire next to the telephone, and he didn't feel like getting up. Honestly!

Said to Anne and Gerald this evening, '*What* time are we leaving on Saturday?'

'Seven, wasn't it?' said Gerald.

'Eight o'clock?' said Anne.

'Four!' I said 'F-O-U-R, FOUR!'

Thursday May 22nd

Strange moment at work today. Glander came across to me and said sneeringly, 'You know that loony mate of yours who was at the party—Thynn, his name is?'

'Yes?' I said, surprised.

'Well,' said Glander, 'a friend of mine told me that, not so very long ago, he saw Mr 'Christian' Thynn, very much the worse for wear, being peeled off the pavement outside the Plough and Bottle, by a couple of the lads in Blue. I thought as he's such a good friend of yours and supposed to be one of Jesus's little sunbeams, perhaps you ought to know about it.'

For one, awful, dark moment, was about to say that Leonard wasn't all that close a friend, and the rest of us in the church weren't like that, but suddenly thought of Anne and Gerald and Kitty and Leonard and Jesus, all waiting to hear what I'd say.

I said, 'I did know about that, Everett. Leonard's one of my best friends, so I hear about most of what happens to him. He's got a problem with drink. I've got a problem with getting things twisted up and making mistakes. All of us in the church have got problems. We're not very good people, but God keeps on forgiving us. Does anyone forgive you for what *you* do, Everett?'

Can't believe *I* said all that! Expected Glander to laugh his head off, but he just frowned and grunted and went back to his desk. Came up to me at the end of the day and *almost* apologised! Who knows—one day . . . ?

No study-group tonight, everybody's getting ready for Saturday. Gerald had a surprise letter today from Andromeda Veal, who stayed with us back in March.

Dear Gerald,

How are you? How is your persunnul problem? I asked muther for one, but she said I must be out of my tiny mined. She is not a soshulist with her own cash. I corled her a thacherite laccy, so she sent me to bed without any mewsli and said I'm afraid I don't think that's very funny. Cum the reverlooshun she'll get hers eh Gerald. When I'm grown up I'm going to live in Rusher. The soshulist ideel is propperly upheld there by Mr Gorgeouschops. I am willing to marry you one

day Gerald as long as I can be a mizz and you
are soshulist with your cash.

Love
Andromeda

P.S. If you wear your persunnul problem out can I
have it?

P.P.S. How's that fashist you live with?

Fashist—I mean, Fascist? Me? Asked Anne where
she would place me in the political spectrum. She said
she thought I was slightly left of gauche . . .

Friday May 23rd

Came through the front door after work today to
overhear Elsie's voice coming from the sitting-room.

'I'm sorry, Gerald, it doesn't matter what you say.
It's over, and that's that! Poor William has suffered
greatly. I feel led to go back to him and that's what
I'm going to do!'

Heard Gerald say, 'But Elsie . . .', then Elsie
came flying out of the room, swooned carefully round
the obstacles in the hall, and slammed dramatically
out of the front door without speaking to me. Found
Gerald sitting in an armchair with his head in his
hands. Went over and put my hand on his shoulder.

I said, 'I know it's hard, Gerald . . .'

Gerald looked up and grinned. 'Telling me it's
hard, dad! It's taken nearly a fortnight to persuade
Elsie that us breaking up is her idea!'

I dunno!

9.30 p.m.

Early to bed tonight so as to be up and ready to go
at 4.00 a.m. I've set the clock for 3.30 a.m., and

that's when we're *all* getting up. Gerald smiled that infuriating smile at me just now as he went off to bed. He thinks I'm going to mess it up—set the clock wrong or something. Anne looks pretty sceptical as well. We shall see. Roll on tomorrow morning. This is the one thing that *won't* go wrong!

10.30 p.m.

Having a little trouble getting to sleep because of worrying about waking up.

11.30 p.m.

Still can't get to sleep. Bit worried now. If I don't go off soon I shall sleep right through the alarm. Must try not to try to relax.

12.15 a.m.

Still awake! Only three and a half hours until the alarm goes off!

12.19 a.m.

Dozed off for one and a half minutes. Dreamt I was awake, and woke up worried about not being asleep.

1.00 a.m.

Too late to think about sleeping now, I must stay awake until 3.30. I must!! Going down to the kitchen to drink coffee.

2.00 a.m.

Still awake! Eyes heavy and blurred—all I want to do is sleep. Hour and a half to go. Mustn't lie down—that would be fatal!

2.45 a.m.

I think I'm going to make it. Feel like death but I'm still asleep—I mean awake.

3.00 a.m.

Good as made it, can't stop yawning but swill atake wade awike . . .

3.29 a.m.

Made it! That'll show 'em. Just sitting in the

armchair for a moment till the alarm goes off dun it! What a trium. . . .

Saturday May 24th

11.00 a.m.

There are times when my family is insufferable!

Anne and Gerald woke me at ten o'clock, and pretended to be very upset because we hadn't made an early start. Gerald said I might at least have gone to bed and *tried* to sleep instead of sitting up all night and dozing off in the armchair. Anne said it was no use my having a quiet-time because God had set off for Wetbridge hours ago. Very funny I don't think. Felt like a dead slug when I tried to get out of my armchair. Feel a lot better now I've had a wash and something to eat. Wetbridge here we come! We're meeting the others down there. Must make sure I take my diary along. I'll be able to sit quietly outside the tent each evening and record the events and revelations of the day. Can't wait!

10.00 p.m.

Arrived at 'Let God Spring into Royal Acts of Harvest Growth' around mid-afternoon. Anne and Gerald and I erected our new 'Tornado-Tough' frame tent in no time, despite high winds and sheeting rain. After checking out the toilets, we walked up to the shop. Passed our magnificent new tent, standing tall and proud in the face of the gale. A little further on, our magnificent new tent passed us, flying through the air like a huge, loony, red and blue sail. Caught it eventually, just outside Richard and Doreen Cook's 'Super-Safari-complete-Comfort-Vacation-Van. Could see Richard inside, drinking tea and reading a bible in the warm. He nodded and smiled and mouthed the words 'Praise the Lord' at me, as I wrestled with my horrible pile of soggy canvas.

Mouthed something back.

Everything soaked! Down to Wetbridge launderette to dry it all. Too late to pitch the tent again when we got back. Went to the 'Let God Spring into Royal Acts of Harvest Growth' office, where a wild-eyed person (who kept saying this was the last year she'd do it) gave us the key to a tiny refrigerated cow-shed, where we're about to stay the night in strange contorted positions.

Sunday May 25th

Down to Wetbridge launderette with clothes soaked by rain coming in through holes in the refrigerated cow-shed. Surprising number of people down there at 7.30 in the morning. One couple who'd spent the night in six inches of water, were anxious to

get back in time for the marriage fulfilment seminar. Seemed a bit desperate really.

Got back and pitched the tent again. Drove pegs through anything that flapped.

Off to the first Celebration this evening with our church group. Relieved Leonard Thynn of a three-pint can of bitter and two bottles of Valpolicella on the way. Explained to him what this kind of Celebration means.

Pleased to see Gerald concentrating hard during the talk. Turned out all his mental energies had gone into working out that Lyndon Bowring was an anagram of 'Born lying down'. Got a bit annoyed with him.

Monday May 26th

Forgot to put clothes away properly last night. All soaked. Down to Wetbridge launderette again. They should have a seminar *there*.

Pete Meadows spoke tonight. Gerald said afterwards, 'Now that was a really good talk, Dad.'

Guiltily confessed that I'd spent most of the time working out that Pete Meadows is an anagram of 'Sweated poem'.

Tuesday May 27th

Back from the Wetbridge launderette this morning to find deaf old Mrs Thynn waiting to tell me how disappointed she was that they hadn't had the chance to save anyone from drowning in her seminar yet.

Stared blankly at her.

'But aren't you in the house to house visitation seminar?' I asked.

'That's right,' she said, mouth to mouth resuscitation.'

Honestly! You'd think Leonard would have explained, wouldn't you?

Some problems over *my* seminar this morning. Was to be in Marquee 9, but had been changed to Marquee 6, only Marquee 6 had blown down, so Marquee 9's seminar was moved to Marquee 14, and the new Marquee 6's seminar was moved back to Marquee 9, only, by now, Marquee 9 had also blown down. Our group ended up wandering disconsolately round the site, looking for an empty marquee, and discussing stability in the church as we went.

Overheard two fellow campers in a local shop later on, while I was waiting to buy fruit-gums for the evening talk. One said the bad weather and the tents blowing down was God's way of saying that these huge gatherings were wrong. The other said it was God's way of testing our perseverance in something that was unquestionably *right*. The old local chap behind the counter interrupted them to say that it always 'bloody rained' down here at this time of the year, and he couldn't understand why they 'kept on 'aving it!'

Wednesday May 28th

Same good old crowd down at Wetbridge launderette this morning. Asked everybody if they'd come to 'Let God Spring into Royal Acts of Harvest Growth' again. They all said they would, because the church thrives under persecution.

Back to the site. Went down for a wash. Funny washing in front of strangers every morning. Feel obliged to be a bit more thorough than usual, in case they think I don't wash enough. The water's so *cold*, despite the fact that the taps are labelled 'C' and 'H'.

154

Gerald says that 'C' stands for 'Cold', and 'H' stands for 'Horribly Cold'.

Thursday May 29th

What a night! Felt as if Giant Haystacks and Big Daddy were shaking our tent in shifts all night. About 2.00 a.m. I said to Anne, 'One of us ought to get out and check the guys and pegs, you know.'

Anne said, 'I agree absolutely. One of us quite definitely should. Yes, one of us should certainly get out and do that.'

Rather obvious snore from Gerald's compartment at this point.

Got up eventually and crawled into the darkness to face Giant Haystacks and Big Daddy. Everything secure. Anne and Gerald fast asleep when I got back. Had two nightmares when I finally got to sleep. In the first, I died and went to heaven, and found it was just like 'Let God Spring into Royal Acts of Harvest Growth'. Woke terrified.

In the second, I died and went to hell, and it was just like 'Let God Spring into Royal Acts of Harvest Growth'. Woke up sweating, and got up early to start collecting stuff for the launderette.

Talked to lots of nice people this morning from lots of different denominations. Had a really great chat in the cafe. Had to stop, unfortunately, or we'd have been late for the seminar on unity.

Friday May 30th

Everything dry this morning! Rather missed the usual launderette trip. Nearly went anyway . . .

Asked Anne this afternoon if she'd enjoyed it all.

She said, 'Oh, yes. Despite everything, it's good to be among all these people who are doing their best to do what God tells them. We're a funny old crowd though, aren't we?'

'Yes,' I thought, 'we certainly are that.'

Silently asked God to show me what really mattered in this strange world of tents and caravans, and Big-tops blowing down, and Celebrations and Christians and cold water and foul weather. As I opened my eyes, a figure passed our tent on the road. It carried a huge wooden mallet. The walk was a plodding, weary one. The young man was dishevelled and grimy. He'd probably been up for the last twenty-four hours at least, working all night in the wind and the rain to save some of the marquee tents. There was the faintest of nightlights still shining in his eyes as he walked. Somehow knew the weather would never quite put that light out.

'There you are,' God seemed to say, 'That's what it's all about.'

It was a steward.

Saturday May 31st

Camp communion today. As we sat waiting for the bread and wine to come round, couldn't help looking at Leonard and Richard and Gerald and Anne and Edwin and the others, and wondering why God's brought us all together. I'm glad he did, though. Felt quite a lump in my throat as I saw old Thynn screwing his eyes tight shut as he took the cup in his hands, and sipped his problem and its solution.

Talking of Leonard—that reminds me. Straight after this I'm going to grab him and make him tell me why he's been borrowing our blinking cat. . . .

You can read more from Adrian Plass's private journals each month in **Christian Family** magazine.

'The Sacred Diary of Adrian Plass' features in each issue of Britain's leading Christian magazine on home and family life. **Christian Family** brings straight-talking and biblical thinking on:

- **MARRIAGE**   From communication to ambition, unemployment to work pressures, we tackle the areas that are the heartbeat of a couple's life together.

- **PARENTING**   Helping mums, dads and youngsters grow together. From toddlers to teens, potties to peer pressure, we address the stress and growing pains. And emphasize the fun!

- **SOCIETY**   Informing you about the world around—from abortion and pornography to secular humanism—we show how it's possible to build a God-centred home in the modern 1980s.

All this and much more each month in **Christian Family** magazine—a year's subscription for only £12.30*. You can make sure of your copy by returning the coupon below.

....

Yes, I'd like to receive **Christian Family** magazine, starting with the.............issue. Please send details of payment with my first copy.

NAME..

ADDRESS ....

....

.... POSTCODE..........

* UK rates only. European rates: £15. Rest of the World: £17

Please return this coupon to: **Christian Family**
Magazine
37 Elm Road
NEW MALDEN
Surrey KT3 3HB

THE GROWING UP PAINS OF ADRIAN PLASS

Adrian Plass

When TV viewers in the south tune into 'Company', they can eavesdrop on a few friends enjoying some late night conversation around a kitchen table. For Adrian Plass, the programme is a landmark in his Christian life. With disarming frankness and irresistible humour, he unfolds his own story and that of some of the programme's memorable guests, such as David Watson, cleaning lady Jo Williams and Auschwitz survivor, Rabbi Hugo Grynn.

OFF THE CHURCH WALL

Rob Portlock

A hilarious collection of cartoons by Rob Portlock, depicting the unusual ways in which people choose to behave in church!

THE HORIZONTAL EPISTLES OF ANDROMEDA VEAL
Illustrated by Dan Donovan

Adrian Plass

Adrian Plass, diary-writer *sans pareil* returns! This time he finds much to amuse him in the letters of Andromeda Veal, precocious eleven year old daughter of a Greenham woman, and shrewd commentator on her local church and the wider world.

Andromeda is in hospital with an undisclosed complaint. She seizes her chance to write all those letters that had to wait before – to, 'Gorgeous Chops', 'Ray Gun', 'Rabbit' Runcie, the Pope, and even Cliff Richard.

At the same time her friends of Sacred Diary fame write to her: Gerald with his mysterious 'persunnul problem', Mrs. Flushpool, Leonard Thin, and also the local MP who vows that she 'can be sick in our hands'! She is also the lucky recipient of letters from conscientious Bible student Charles Cooke who finds 15 texts for every word of 'I hope you get better soon', and a large Christian organization whose aims appear to change from letter to letter. Of course Andromeda's illness gives her a chance to think more seriously about God too, even to the extent of writing him a letter.

All of this is interspersed with new diary entries from Adrian Plass' inimitable diary writer and Dan Donovan's hilarious illustrations.